4

by

FRED GALLAGHER

"leave it to seraphim" comics written by

SARAH GALLAGHER

"shirt guy dom" comics by

DOMINIC NGUYEN

www.megatokyo.com

cmxmanga.com

For Sarah, with love.

メガトーキョー
megatokyo
④

SECOND PRINTING

Fred Gallagher & Larry Berry – Design
Jim Chadwick – Editor

ISBN:1-4012-1126-7
ISBN-13: 978-1-4012-1126-4

CONTENTS

MT_vol_4_fr33talk.txt

Hi again, welcome to Megatokyo volume 4.

If you are a *Megatokyo* reader and have been following the comic online, then you should be familiar with the content of this book. It contains Chapter 5 and Chapter 6 (that's comics 526 to 742 -- February 2004 to August 2005) as well as most of the other content that appeared during that time. These include "Dead Piro Days," One Shot Episodes, hiccups and even (shudder) "Shirt Guy Dom" strips. There was no "omake" (extra, or bonus material) at the end of Chapter 5, but I have expanded and revised the Omake I did for Chapter 6 which you will find at the end of this book. At 240 pages, this is the thickest *Megatokyo* book yet. Not that size really matters.

For the past three volumes, the extra material in these books has always been related in some way to Piro and Largo's "Endgame" adventures. Since these adventures had seeped into the comic at the end of Chapter 7 (which I was producing at the same time I was working on this book), I found myself wanting to do something different.

The Chapter 6 omake, "Circuity," was an experiment with placing the characters in a far more serious story, and I thought it turned out to be a very moving piece. The only problem with it was some of its rather specific fan-work nature (in referencing one of my favorite anime series of all time) and the fact that it was too short -- the end of it felt very rushed. I decided to take what I had done and revise, rework and expand it. By freeing the story of its fan-work constraints, I found I was able to change the Circuity world into something more unique and complimentary to the ideas I was trying to expand upon.

It is now a more complete work that stands well on its own. I'm very happy with the results, and I hope you enjoy the "rewound" version as well.

If none of what I wrote above makes any sense at all, and this is the first time you've ever picked up a *Megatokyo* book, I suppose you might appreciate some sort of explanation as to what all this is about.

MT_vol_4_fr33talk.txt

Megatokyo is an online webcomic that Rodney Caston (Largo) and I (Piro) started back in August 2001. It is the story of Piro and Largo, two friends who fly to Japan on a whim and find themselves stranded and unable to afford the trip home. In 2002, Rodney left the project and I have been working solo on it since. New comics are posted every Monday, Wednesday and Friday (usually) and each installment is (supposedly) designed to stand on its own. When collected together, the intent is that they read as a cohesive story.

Since *Megatokyo* started, the website has grown a sizeable readership and has become home to a fairly active fan community. I'm really not sure how many people read *Megatokyo*, but I do know that it takes six servers to manage everything -- Makoto, Mishio, Nayuki, Akiko, Sayuri and Mai. The hosting bills are also easy to understand, never mind what it costs for food, snacks, manga and cable TV for the server harem.

I've used this FreeTalk section in the past three books to try to summarize the *Megatokyo* story up to the point at which each book starts. The summary I wrote for Volume 3 was painful to read, and I felt that it really did not touch on everything that needed to be covered. For this book, I looked back on five chapters and 500+ comics and decided that trying to condense all of that into two little pages of text was a hopeless task.

So, what to do? If this is your first exposure to *Megatokyo*, how do I set you off on the right foot?

Ideally, reading the story itself is far better than any synopsis I could write (and far more enjoyable). The first three books are the most convenient way to do this, but you can also read it online at www.megatokyo.com -- every *Megatokyo* comic, including the ones in this book, is there for the viewing.

You could also just dive into this book and figure things out as you go. That's actually not as bad an idea as it sounds. While there is a lot that happens in the first three books, it is in the chapters contained in this book that things really start moving.

MT_vol_4_fr33talk.txt

So, if you're gonna just dive in, I'll give you a few quick notes on what's up so you aren't totally lost.

It's pretty obvious that Piro and Largo are still stuck in Japan and are no closer to finding a way home. Oddly enough, this issue doesn't seem to be too important. Piro has a job at an anime and game store called MegaGamers and the boss is letting them stay in the top-floor apartment. He's getting to know a young voice actress named Kimiko who recently landed a part doing the voice of one of his favorite characters in an upcoming game. As long as he can keep Largo more or less out of trouble, life isn't too bad, even if the advice his conscience is giving him seems somewhat odd.

Largo has determined that Kimiko's friend Erika is the focus of some kind of vast, undead horde. He has successfully beaten off the infiltration of advance scouts and penetrating attacks on the digital plane, but how long can he keep this horde from overwhelming them?

That should be enough to get you started. If you do make it through this book and don't have a strong desire to add it to the burn pile, you can either pick up the first three books or head online to catch up with things from the beginning. Then, you can head online to comic number 743 and pick up where this book leaves off.

Thanks for reading, and I hope you enjoy this book as much as I've enjoyed pulling it together :)

piro

chapter 5:
"color depth"

<SO... YOU CAN'T SEE ANY COLORS AT ALL?>

<OH, NO, I SEE COLORS. SOMETIMES I SEE A HINT OF COLOR AT THE EDGES OF THINGS, OTHER TIMES EVERYTHING IS MISTY PASTELS.>

<FOR THE MOST PART THOUGH, EVERYTHING IS JUST SHADES OF GRAY.>

<THAT'S TERRIBLE.>

<WELL, NOT REALLY. IT'S BETTER THAN NOT SEEING ANY COLOR AT ALL.>

<ARE YOU SURE? DOESN'T SEEING COLOR SOMETIMES BUT NOT ALL THE TIME MAKE YOU SAD?>

<WOULDN'T IT BE BETTER IF YOU JUST COULDN'T SEE ANY COLOR AT ALL?>

<WELL, NO, NOT REALLY...>

<NO... HOW WOULD THAT BE BETTER?>

<WHAT ABOUT ME? WHAT COLOR AM I?>

<CUT!!>

<NANASAWA, WHAT ARE YOU DOING?>

<...?>

<CAN WE PLEASE STICK TO THE SCRIPT?>
<BUT THAT WAS THE SCRIPT.>
<SORTA.>
<VERY FUNNY. CAN WE MOVE ON NOW?>
<SORRY, SORRY.>
<I'M NOT REALLY VERY GOOD AT THIS.>
<I WISH I COULD TURN MY FEELINGS ON AND OFF LIKE I'M SUPPOSED TO.>
PORTLAND'S BES
<IF YOU COULD DO THAT, YOU'D BE A MACHINE, NOT AN ACTRESS.>
<SHOWING REAL EMOTIONS IS GOOD, YOU JUST NEED TO FOCUS AND GET INTO THE MOOD OF THINGS SO THEY ARE THE RIGHT ONES.>
<NORMALLY I'M REALLY A LOT LIKE KOTONE.>
<IT'S JUST THAT I'VE BEEN IN AN ODD MOOD LATELY.>
<I MET THIS GUY...>
<OH GOD.>
<NO, IT'S NOT LIKE THAT.>
<YOU SEE, NOTHING IN THE REAL WORLD WILL EVER LIVE UP TO WHAT I FEEL INSIDE.>
<I CAME TO TERMS WITH THAT A LONG TIME AGO.>
<ACTING AS A CHARACTER IN A STORY GIVES ME A CHANCE TO SHARE THESE FEELINGS WITH OTHERS, ON SOME LEVEL.>
<THIS GUY I MET... HE'S JUST SOMEONE I THINK WOULD UNDERSTAND THAT.>
<AND IT MAKES ME FEEL GOOD KNOWING HE MIGHT.>
<SO... YOU'RE NOT AN "AIRHEAD" TYPE VOICE ACTRESS, YOU'RE MORE THE "REALLY MESSED UP IN THE HEAD" TYPE.>
<I'M SORRY!>
<DON'T BE. I THINK I PREFER THIS.>

<I THINK I JUST FEEL THINGS MORE INTENSELY THAN MOST PEOPLE.>
<I DON'T THINK HOW I FEEL INSIDE CAN REALLY BE COMMUNICATED TO ANYONE.>
<MAYBE IT'S BECAUSE THE FEELINGS I HAVE WORK ONLY IN FANTASIES, NOT THE REAL WORLD.>
<THAT'S WHY I WANT TO BE AN ACTRESS. IT'S A WAY TO LIVE WHAT I FEEL, EVEN IF IT IS JUST PART OF A STORY.>
<THIS GUY I MET... HE'S NOT MY TYPE, HE'S NOT EVEN JAPANESE, BUT I THINK HE'S THE KIND OF PERSON WHO CAN ALMOST UNDERSTAND HOW I FEEL.>
<IT'S ALMOST LIKE I COULD GET A LITTLE CLOSER TO HIM.>
<JUST A LITTLE.>
<EVEN IF IT IS ONLY THROUGH A GAME.>
<I'M SORRY...>
<I'M SURE YOU DON'T WANT TO BE HEARING ANY OF THIS.>
<NO, THAT'S OK.>
<I DON'T REALLY KNOW WHAT TO SAY, BUT IT SOUNDS TO ME LIKE YOU SHOULD STOP BEING SO NEGATIVE AND GIVE THIS GUY MORE OF A CHANCE.>
<HE MIGHT SURPRISE YOU.>
<OH, IT'S REALLY NOTHING THAT SERIOUS. I... BARELY KNOW HIM.>
<BESIDES, I'M SURE HE HAS BETTER THINGS TO DO THAN TO HAVE TO DEAL WITH MY LITTLE QUIRKS.>
THESE PANTS MUST HAVE CAUSED THE STATIC DISCHARGE THAT SET OFF THE FLASH FIRE IN THE REMAINS OF MY B3OWULF CLUSTER .
I MUST REMOVE THEM.
<PIRO-SAN! I USED THE WHOLE EXTINGUISHER! IT'S STILL BURNING!>
ENOUGH WITH THE PANTS!! HELP US PUT THIS OUT!!

I... I THINK... I THINK IT'S FINALLY OUT.
THIS IS OBVIOUSLY THE RESULT OF FAULTY AND/OR INFERIOR COMPONENTS.
I THINK I CAN NAME ONE.
<KYAA!!>
<PIRO-SAN! I'M LATE! I'M LATE FOR SCHOOL!!
<MY HAIR SMELLS LIKE SMOKE! WHAT AM I GONNA DO??
I MUST PROTECT REMAINING COMPONENTS FROM DAMAGE.
<PING, YOU'RE A PLAYSTATION ACCESSORY, YOU DON'T HAVE TO GO TO SCHOOL...>
I DECLARE THIS AREA OVER HERE A ST4TIC FR33 ZONE!
<I HAVE TO CHANGE! WHERE'S MY UNIFORM??>
I MUST REBUILD OUR DEFENSES, WE ARE VULNER-ABLE.
<I'M SO LATE!! YOU AND LARGO-SAN HAVE TO GO OUTSIDE SO I CAN CHANGE!>
KNOCK
KNOCK
NONE OF YOU HAVE TO DO ANYTHING...
CURSES! THE POWER CORDS HAVE ALL MELTED!!
<I KNOW! I'LL PILE UP BOXES SO I CAN HAVE SOME PRIVACY!>
GREAT, THE PSYCHO GOTHIC GAMER CHICK IS HERE.
MAYBE SHE'LL TAKE BOTH OF THEM WITH HER THIS TIME.
<PING! HURRY UP AND GET DRESSED!>
GOOD GOD! LARGO! FOR THE LOVE OF DECENCY PUT SOME PANTS ON!!
SOMEONE OPEN A WINDOW, IT STINKS IN HERE!
LARGO!! THAT THING IS SPARKING! UNPLUG IT!!!
<SORRY ABOUT THAT, PING'S JUS-->
GEEP!
DO YOU STILL NEED A FEW MOMENTS?
I CAN WAIT.

HA.. HA... HAYASAKA-SAN! WHA... WHAT'RE YOU DOING UP HERE?
BRINGING BREAKFAST. COFFEE AND PASTRIES, TO BE EXACT.
OH! OK, I, UH... JUST A SEC...
LARGO! HAYASAKA-SAN IS HERE! PUT A SHIRT ON!
WHY?
BECAUSE SHE BROUGHT DONUTS.
DONUTS? SW33T!!
<PIRO-SAN, THAT ISN'T TOHYA-CHAN AT THE DOOR?>
<NO, IT'S NOT PING.>
<DO YOU THINK SHE WENT TO SCHOOL WITHOUT ME?>
<PING...>
<THIS IS YOUR FAULT!>
<YOU DIDN'T LET ME SLEEP UNTIL WAY TOO LATE LAST NIGHT! THAT'S WHY I DIDN'T WAKE UP IN TIME FOR SCHOOL!>

<MOUUU...>
<SHE PROBABLY KNOCKED ON THE DOOR BUT WE WERE STILL ASLEEP...>
<OH! HAYASAKA-SAN! GOOD MORNING!>
<I'D LOVE TO STAY FOR A DONUT, BUT I'M LATE FOR SCHOOL!>

<TELL PIRO-SAN THAT I'LL COME STRAIGHT BACK AFTER CLASS.>
<BAI BAI!>
SORRY ABOUT THAT.
I KNOW SHE'S A ROBOT AND A PLAYSTATION ACCESSORY, BUT I STILL CAN'T HELP BEING SLIGHTLY DISTURBED BY IT ALL.
BY ALL WHAT?

SORRY ABOUT THE BURNING SMELL. IT HAPPENS WHEN LARGO TRIES TO COOK THINGS.
THAT'S OK.
THANK YOU FOR THE COFFEE AND DONUTS.
YOU'RE WELCOME.
THESE BAKED GOODS HAVE REMARKABLE HEALTH RESTORING QUALITIES.
UHM HM.
SO... WHAT MADE YOU THINK OF COMING UP HERE THIS MORNING?
NO REASON.
OH.
IS IT ME, OR IS HAYASAKA-SAN ACTING KINDA STRANGE?
SOMETHING IS BOTHERING HER, I CAN...
WHAT THE?

THERE'S A HUGE CROWD OUTSIDE THE STORE!
HAYASAKA-SAN, WHAT'S GOING ON?
MANIC UNDO
HAYASAKA-SAN?
UH...
IS THAT YOUR CELL PHONE THAT'S RINGING?
bringbring *bing bing *bringbring *bing
YES.
AREN'T YOU... GONNA ANSWER IT?
IT'S PROBABLY YANAGISAWA WONDERING WHERE WE ARE.
OUR BOSS?
UHN.
BUT... WHAT'S WITH THE CROWD? IS THERE SOME KINDA SPECIAL EVENT AT THE STORE TODAY??
NO IDEA.
MAYBE IT'S SOME SORT OF LIMITED EDITION GAME RELEASE OR SOME-THING!
YOU SHOULD GO DOWN AND HELP HIM.
RIGHT!
MANIC UNDO
bringbring *bing bing *bringbring bing* bringbring bin-
UH...
AREN'T YOU COMING?
YOU GO HAVE FUN. I'LL STAY HERE AND FINISH MY COFFEE.
-CLICK-

<I WONDER WHAT THE CROWD IS HERE FOR?>
<ARE THEY WAITING FOR THE STORE TO OPEN?>
<POOR PIRO-SAN. HE'S GOING TO HAVE A BUSY DAY.>
<I WONDER WHAT HAPPENED TO MIHO-CHAN?>
<IS SHE HOME SICK? WAS SHE JUST GOING TO MEET ME AT SCHOOL?>
<DOESN'T SHE CARE ABOUT ME ANYMORE?>
<I THOUGHT WE WERE FRIENDS...>
<JUNPEI SEE SHIRITSU DAITOU HIGH SCHOOL STUDENT.>
<JUNPEI WANT KNOW WHY STUDENT NOT IN SCHOOL.>
<EEEP!>
<I...I... I'M SORRY! I'M LATE! I'M GOING STRAIGHT TO SCHOOL RIGHT NOW! I'M LATE BECAUSE LARGO-SENSEI SET FIRE TO OUR APARTMENT THIS MORNING AND I HAD TO HELP PUT IT OUT!!>
<LARGO-SENSEI?>
<JUNPEI NOT KNOW L33T MASTER HAVE DAUGHTER.>
<OH, I'M NOT HIS DAUGHTER, WE JUST LIVE TOGETHER.>
<MANY THINGS ABOUT L33T MASTER JUNPEI NOT KNOW.>
<I REALLY HAVE TO GO, I'M LATE FOR CLASS.>

WOW, LOOK AT ALL THESE PEOPLE...
<HEY! LOOK! SOME GUY JUST CAME DOWN FROM UP-STAIRS!>
<HEY!>

<DO YOU WORK HERE?>
<UHM, YEAH.>
<IS HAYASAKA-HIME REALLY IN THE STORE RIGHT NOW??>
<HAYASAKA... HIME?>
<WHEN WILL THE STORE OPEN?? WILL YOU OPEN SOON??>

<WILL SHE BE SIGNING AUTO-GRAPHS??>
<DO YOU KNOW HER? IS SHE STILL THE SAME??>
<PIRO!!!>
<IS SHE STILL BEAUTIFUL?? SHE ISN'T REALLY BROKEN, IS SHE???>
<I...>
<WHA...>
<WILL SHE SIGN ONE OF MY LIMITED EDITION HAYASAKA DOLLS?>
<WILL SHE BE DOING ANY SPECIAL EVENTS??>

<EXCUSE ME...>
<EXCUSE ME.>
<WHERE THE BLAZES HAVE YOU BEEN?>
<GET INSIDE, NOW!>

<SHE WAS PRACTICALLY A HOUSEHOLD NAME IN JAPAN A FEW YEARS AGO.>
<AND YOU CALL YOURSELF AN ANIME FAN.>
<SHE WAS? WHAT DID SHE DO?>
MANIC UNDO RECORDS
MEGA
<OK, HOW LONG HAVE YOU BEEN INTO ANIME?>
<ABOUT SEVEN YEARS OR SO, I THINK.>
<REMEMBER A POPULAR ANIME CALLED "GIRL PHASE?" IT WAS REAL HOT A FEW YEARS AGO.>
<OF COURSE! I HAVE ALL THREE BOX SETS AND ALL THE OAVS.>
<NOW, REMEMBER, MOEKO, THE MAIN CHARACTER?>
<YEAH! SHE WAS REALLY CUTE! I EVEN HAVE ONE OF THOSE FULL-SIZE MOEKO BODY PILLOWS!>
<RIGHT. SO, DO YOU REMEMBER MOEKO'S VOICE ACTRESS?>
<HAYASAKA ERIKA, OF COURSE!>
<HAYASAKA WAS LIKE THE CUTEST SEIYUU EVER!>
<I USED TO HAVE A LIFE SIZE POSTER OF HER HANGING ON MY DOOR UNTIL...>
<LARGO...>
MANIC
MANIC
<LEMME KNOW WHEN YOU'RE FINISHED. THERE'S A BIG CROWD OUT THERE WE STILL HAVE TO DEAL WITH.>
<OH, AND YOU MIGHT WANT TO KEEP THE BIT ABOUT THE BODY PILLOW TO YOURSELF.>
MANIC

THIS IS NOT GOOD.
VIOLENCE IS BREWING.
I CAN FEEL IT.
PIRO MAY BE LOST TO US. I DO NOT THINK HE MADE IT TO THE BREACH.
THE FOOL.
WE ARE TRAPPED HERE. WE CANNOT GET OUT.
SOON THEY WILL COME.
ALL IS NOT LOST. OUR DEFENSES ARE WEAK, BUT WE...
ERR...
I DO NOT WANT, NOR DO I NEED, YOU TO PROTECT ME.

WHATEVER.
DOESN'T MATTER. WE ARE BOTH TRAPPED HERE.
I AM NOT TRAPPED.
I CAN LEAVE IF I WANT.
AH...
WHA--!!

RATTLE
RATTLE
RATTLE
CLINK
<IT'S LOCKED.>
<YOU SURE?>
RATTLE
RATTLE
<YEAH, IT WON'T BUDGE.>
<I GUESS WE CAN'T SNEAK IN THIS WAY.>
<ARE THERE ANY OTHER DOORS WE CAN TRY?>
<NOT UP HERE. COME'ON.>
HM.
I SEEM TO BE INCAPABLE OF MOVEMENT.
...GOMEN.

<LOOKS LIKE I MISSED THE FIRST CLASS PERIOD.>
<THAT WAS REALLY LAME.>
<ERI, CAN I BORROW YOUR NOTES?>
<MIHO-CHAN.>
<SHE'S NOT HERE.>
<IS SHE SICK?>
<DID SHE STAY HOME BECAUSE SHE'S SICK AGAIN?>
<WOAH!! WHO IS THAT!!>
<OH WOW!!>
<WHY DIDN'T SHE CALL ME? SHE PROMISED...>
GOOD MORNING CLASS.
MR. SETO HAD A LITTLE... ACCIDENT THIS MORNING.
<KYAA!!>
ALL'S RIGHT WITH THE WORLD
SLAM!
<HE'S GONNA TEACH THE CLASS IN ENGLISH?>
<WHO CARES??>
<ISN'T THAT...>
<FROM YESTERDAY'S SCENARIO?>
I'LL BE YOUR SUBSTITUTE TEACHER FOR SOCIAL STUDIES THIS MORNING.
I'M SURE WE'LL HAVE LOTS OF FUN TOGETHER.

<KO...>
<KOTONE...>
<AFTER EVERYTHING HE HAD BEEN THROUGH, AFTER STRUGGLING SO HARD...>
<HE...HE CAN'T BE GONE...>
<IT'S NOT FAIR.>
<I'M SO SORRY, KOTONE. WE DID EVERYTHING WE COULD FOR HIM, HE JUST COULDN'T...>
<WHY DID HE HAVE TO DIE?!>
<HE WAS SO CONFUSED! HE DIDN'T UNDER-STAND WHAT HAD HAPPENED TO HIM! IT'S NOT FAIR!!>

<OK...>
<I...>
<THAT...>
<THAT WAS PERFECT. DEAD ON.>
<THANK YOU, NANASAWA-SAN, GOOD JOB.>
<OK, WE'VE MADE A LOT OF PROGRESS THIS MORNING.>
<NEXT WE'LL TACKLE SCENE 36 AND ITS VARIATIONS.>
<ARE YOU OK?>
<I REALLY HATE THE SCENARIO WHERE HER KITTY DIES.>
<POOR BURN. IT'S ALMOST TOO SAD.>
<I'M GLAD HE ONLY DIES IN ONE OF THE SCENARIOS.>
<UHM... MAYBE WE SHOULD TAKE A BREAK.>
<YOU'RE DOING REALLY WELL, BUT I'M WORRIED THAT YOU ARE...>
<THANK YOU, MATSUI-SAN, BUT THAT'S OK.>
<I ALWAYS TEAR UP WHEN I DO SAD PARTS. IT JUST SORTA WELLS UP AND I CAN'T STOP IT.>
<SCENE 36 ISN'T QUITE SO SAD. I COULD USE THAT RIGHT NOW.>
<SHALL WE CONTINUE?>

HOW DID THIS HAPPEN.

YOU SUFFER FROM FATAL WEAKNESSES IN THE DIGITAL PLANE.
THE WHAT?

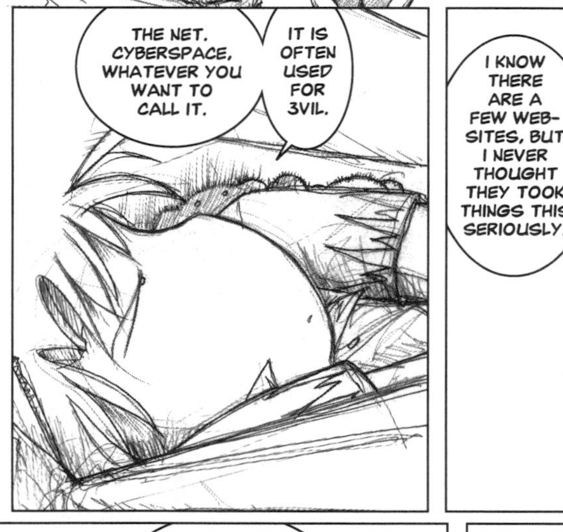
THE NET. CYBERSPACE, WHATEVER YOU WANT TO CALL IT.
IT IS OFTEN USED FOR 3VIL.

I KNOW THERE ARE A FEW WEB-SITES, BUT I NEVER THOUGHT THEY TOOK THINGS THIS SERIOUSLY.

SO, MISTER COMPUTER EXPERT, HOW CAN I FIX THIS "FATAL WEAKNESS?"

SOMETHING IS AT THE DOOR.

SOMETHING IS THERE.
I DON'T HEAR ANY-THING.
I CAN F33L IT.
THERE'S NOTHING--
SHHH!!!
WOW.
THOSE ARE A LOT SOFTER THAN I THOUGHT THEY'D BE.
RATTLE RATTLE RATTLE RATTLE RATTLE RATTLE
<MY GOD, WHAT WAS THAT??>
<IT KINDA SOUNDED LIKE A TRUCK RUNNING INTO THE BUILDING.>

JUNPEI HEAR L33T MASTER CRY OUT IN GREAT PAIN!!
KEYLESS ENTER!!!
CRACK
WHAM!
<JUNPEI SORRY. NOT MEAN INTERRUPT HONORABLE MELEE.>
<JUNPEI COME BACK LATER.>
<NO, THAT'S OK. I THINK WE'RE DONE.>
FULL OF NOT SOFT THINGS.
CAN'T... FEEL TOES...

<I CAN'T BELIEVE THAT HAYASAKA-SAN IS... HAYASAKA ERIKA.>
<SO YOU KEEP SAYING.>
MANIC UNDO

<BUT... BUT... WHY IS SHE WORKING HERE??>
<WHAT DO YOU KNOW ABOUT HER DISAPPEARANCE?>
<WELL, THERE WERE LOTS OF STORIES, BUT NO ONE KNEW WHAT TO BELIEVE.>
MEGA GAMERS

<YOU HEARD THE STORY ABOUT HER LAST STAGE APPEARANCE, RIGHT?>
<THE ONE WHERE SHE WALKED ON STAGE AND TOLD THE AUDIENCE THAT EVERYTHING THEY LOVED IS A LIE?>
<YEAH, THAT ONE.>
<THAT ACTUALLY HAPPENED. EVERYTHING ELSE YOU'VE PROBABLY HEARD ISN'T TRUE.>
<I THINK HER HANDLERS STARTED THE FIRST RUMORS.>
<SHE WAS PREGNANT, SHE HAD A NERVOUS BREAKDOWN, SHE HAD A DRUG PROBLEM, SHE WAS A VIOLENT PSYCHOTIC...>

<EVERYTHING BUT THE TRUE STORY. WHAT REALLY HAPPENED WASN'T QUITE SO "ENTERTAINING.">
<DAMMIT, HAYASAKA, WHERE THE HELL ARE YOU?>
<SHE'S UPSTAIRS.>

<SHE'S WHERE?>
<UPSTAIRS IN OUR APARTMENT. SHE BROUGHT COFFEE AND DONUTS FOR LARGO AND ME THIS MORNING.>
MEGA GAMERS

<I'VE BEEN TRYING TO FIND OUT WHERE SHE IS FOR A HALF HOUR AND IT DIDN'T OCCUR TO YOU TO TELL ME THIS???>
<I THOUGHT YOU KNEW.>
MEGA GAMERS

WO4|-|!

OOF!
FUMP!

L33T MASTER.
JUNPEI SENT TO BRING MASTER TO TEACH CLASS.
YET...

JUNPEI SENSE L33T MASTER FACE MANY UNFINISHED BATTLES.

DUDE. YOU BROKE THE DOOR. THAT WAS THE LAST DEFENSE WE HAD.
JUNPEI SORRY. WILL SCHEDULE REPAIR.

JUNPEI PLACE MANY OBJECTS TO BLOCK DOOR AS L33T MASTER REQUESTED.
L33T MASTER WILL BE LATE FOR CLASS. MUST LEAVE SOON.
CHILL A CYCLE. I MUST CHECK ENEMY CHATTER.

DUDE.
WITH YOUR NINJ4 TRAINING... CAN YOU READ ANY OF THIS 3VIL?

IT IS DISCUSSION ABOUT DISCOVERY OF LONG MISSING, FAMOUS IDOL.
THEY ARE VERY EXCITED. MANY SEEM TO BE IN CROWD OUTSIDE OF STORE.
HMM...

SO, THE DARK ONE HAS MOBILIZED THESE MINIONS BY PROMISING THEM THE APPEARANCE OF SOME HISTORICAL "IDOL" THEY WORSHIP.
THEY SAY WILL MAINTAIN VIGIL AT STORE UNTIL FAMOUS IDOL APPEAR.

IF WE KNEW WHAT THIS "IDOL" WAS, WE COULD TRICK THEM INTO WORSHIPING IT, AND CONTROL THEM.
ONE SAY HE HAVE NAKED PHOTOS OF IDOL ON WEBSITE.

THE HELL HE DOES...
NAKED PHOTOS?
LET'S SEE WHAT THIS "IDOL" LOOKS LIKE!
WAIT. ALL SAY PHOTOS OLD HOAX. NOT REAL.

WE'VE BEEN SEARCHING ALL NIGHT. WHAT COULD HAVE HAPPENED TO HER?
I GUESS WE BETTER CALL IN AND REPORT HER MISSING.
I'M GONNA GET IN SO MUCH TROUBLE FOR THIS.
THEY... THEY MIGHT EVEN TAKE AWAY MY GAMESTOP DISCOUNT CARD.
WOW, THERE SURE ARE A LOT OF CRYING CHILDREN IN THIS PARK.
<MUH... MUH...>
<MOMMIEEE!?!>
<WAHH!!! FIPPO KILLED SOMETHING!!>
<DON'T BE SILLY! FIPPO IS A STUFFED TOY! HE CAN'T HURT ANYTHING!>
<OHHH!!!>
POP
POP
POP
POP
POP! POP! POP!
<WAH!!>
<MOMMIE!!!>
HEY!! IS THAT...? IT IS! WE FOUND HER! SHE'S ALIVE! I'M SAVED!!
SQUEEK SQUEEEK!!
WAIT...
DID SHE JUST DUMP THAT KID'S ICE CREAM CONE ON THE GROUND?
SQU--

HEY!!
SQUEEK! SQUEEK!

WHAT ARE YOU...
HEY!!

SHE RAN AWAY?
WHY DID SHE RUN AWAY?
DON'T YOU THINK SERAPHIM IS ACTING... KIND OF STRANGE?
SQUEEH.

OK. YOU MADE ALL THOSE BOXES FALL ON HER, THEN WHEN WE WOKE UP, SHE WAS GONE.
I WONDER, IF WHEN THAT CRATE LANDED ON HER, MAYBE SOMETHING IN HER HEAD GOT RATTLED.
MAYBE SHE HAS AMNESIA.

SQUEEEEEEK!!
NO, WAIT.

SHE'S NOT GONNA BE ABLE TO RAT ON US IF SHE DOESN'T REMEMBER ANYTHING, SO RELAX.
BESIDES, IT LOOKS LIKE THIS LITTLE MEMORY LOSS MIGHT GO BACK A LONG WAY.
I HAVEN'T SEEN HER ACT LIKE THIS IN YEARS.

SEEMS LIKE SHE'S BACK TO HER OLD SELF.
I SHOULDA DROPPED A CRATE ON HER A LONG TIME AGO.
THIS IS GONNA BE FUN.

WHAT'RE YOU ALL WORKED UP ABOUT?
SERAPHIM HASN'T ALWAYS BEEN A PRISSY LITTLE GOODY-GOODY, YOU KNOW.

IN FACT, YOU COULD SAY SHE WAS A VERY BAD LITTLE ANGEL.
CLIENTS GET ONLY ONE CEA OP WHO ADVISES THEM ON ALL SIDES OF THEIR MORAL CONFLICTS. THEY ARE BOTH GOOD AND BAD CONSCIENCES.
WHEN SERAPHIM IS GOOD SHE'S GOOD. WHEN SHE'S BAD, SHE'S REALLY BAD.

OF COURSE, MY MISSIONS DON'T REQUIRE THAT KIND OF DUALITY.
FUN IS FUN, THERE IS NO GOOD OR BAD.
EVEN AS A TEMP, YOU SHOULD KNOW THIS.

SPEAKING OF WHICH, WHATEVER HAPPENED TO YOUR CLIENT?

YOUR CLIENT'S MORAL CONFLICTS USUALLY RESULT IN PHYSICAL PAIN.
DON'T YOU THINK YOU SHOULD KEEP A CLOSER EYE ON HIM?

HM. THERE ARE NO N3KKID PIX, BUT THESE WEBSITES ALL HAVE PICTURES OF A HUMAN FEMALE IN VARIOUS UNUSUAL CEREMONIAL OUTFITS.
COULD THIS HUMAN FEMALE BE THE "IDOL" THAT THEY SEEK?
NO, IT'S NOT POSSIBLE.
THE UNDEAD LUST AFTER LIVING FLESH. THEY DO NOT WORSHIP IT.
PERHAPS SHE IS SOME SORT OF HIGH UNDEAD PRIESTESS.
AND THE "IDOL" MUST BE THIS ABSTRACT, CARTOONISH THING PICTURED BEHIND HER.

JUNPEI!
YES, L33T MASTER.
WE MUST GO DOWN INTO THE CROWD AND INVESTIGATE THIS FURTHER.
AND JUST HOW DO YOU PLAN TO GET OUT? YOUR FRIEND HERE BLOCKED THE DOOR WITH THE FRIDGE AND THE STOVE.

THAT'S WHAT WINDOWS AND MAD NINJ4 SKILLZ ARE FOR.

YOU AREN'T SERIOUSLY THINKING OF GOING OUT THE WINDOW.

IT IS THE LEAST EXPECTED ROUTE.
THEREFORE, THE SAFEST.

JUNPEI! LET'S GO.
YES, L33T MASTER.
BUT THIS IS THE THIRD FLOOR...

RELAX.
WE'LL BE BACK.

AHH!

WH... WHERE'D THEY GO??
<OH MY GOD, LOOK UP!!>
<IT'S HER! IT'S HER!!>

<HAYASAKA-HIME!>
<HAYASAKA-HIME!!>
<ERI-RIN!>
<ERI-RIN!!>
<IS THAT REALLY HER?>
<WOOO!!>
WOOSH
SLAM!!
BAM! BAM! -CRACK-
<THERE! GOT IT.>
<WE'RE IN.>
-CREEEEEAK-
<OOF.>
<NOW, HOLD THE LADDER STE-- >
<AW, CRAP.>
<BOSS-SAN!!>
<OK... LOOKS LIKE HAYASAKA IS DOING JUST FINE.>
<DON'T KNOW WHY I WORRIED ABOUT HER... OW.>
MANIC

<UHM...>
<HAYASAKA-SAN?>
<IS THAT OLD FOOL ALL RIGHT?>
<I THINK SO.>
<I'M OK, NOTHING TO WORRY ABOUT.>
<UH...>
<ARE YOU OK? YOU LOOK UPSET.>
<Y'KNOW...>
<I COULD, LIKE, GO OUTSIDE AND TELL THEM YOU AREN'T HERE.>
<TELL THEM TO GO AWAY, OR SOMETHIN'.>
<JUST LIKE THAT.>
<OI, YANAGISAWA. ARE YOU SURE YOU'RE OK?>
<I'M JUST GONNA LAY HERE AND STARE AT THE CEILING FOR A WHILE. IT'S SUCH A PEACEFUL CEILING.>

IT IS JUST AS I THOUGHT.
MEGAGAMERS
THESE MINIONS VIEW PIRO'S CO-WORKER AS A PHYSICAL MANIFESTATION OF THIS "IDOL" THEY WORSHIP.
SHE BEARS A STRONG RESEMBLANCE TO THE HIGH PRIESTESS PICTURED ON THOSE WEBSITES.
I DON'T BELIEVE THIS TO BE RANDOM CHANCE.
YET I SENSE NO EVIL PURPOSE IN HER.
THIS IS SOMETHING FROM HER PAST.
IT IS NOT SOMETHING SHE SEEMS TO WELCOME.
JUNPEI, WHEN AM I SUPPOSED TO TEACH MY CLASS?
CLASS START FIVE MINUTES.
IT IS TIME FOR GREAT TEACHER LARGO TO GIVE HIS FIRST TEST.

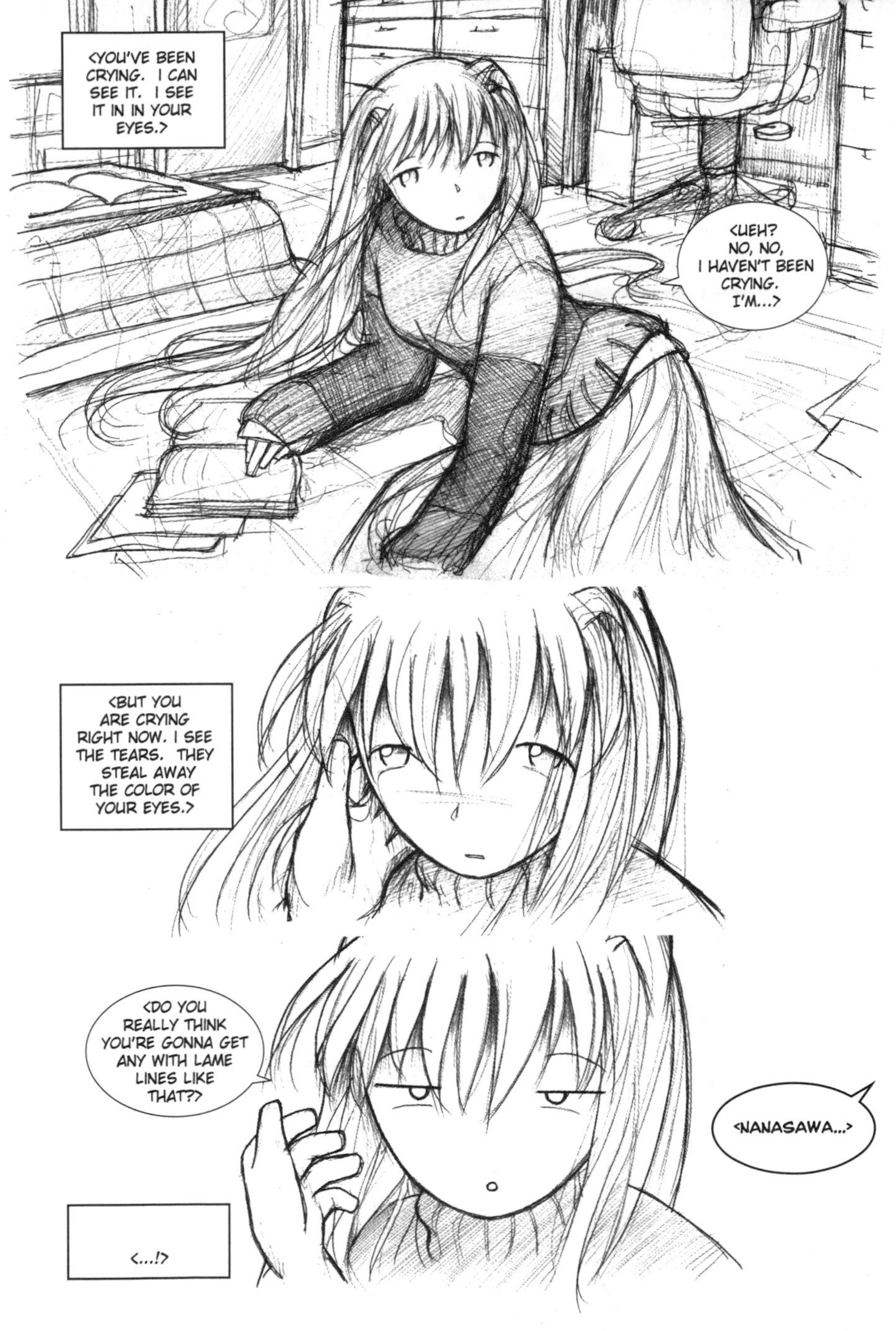
<YOU'VE BEEN CRYING. I CAN SEE IT. I SEE IT IN IN YOUR EYES.>
<UEH? NO, NO, I HAVEN'T BEEN CRYING. I'M...>
<BUT YOU ARE CRYING RIGHT NOW. I SEE THE TEARS. THEY STEAL AWAY THE COLOR OF YOUR EYES.>
<DO YOU REALLY THINK YOU'RE GONNA GET ANY WITH LAME LINES LIKE THAT?>
<NANASAWA...>
<...!>

<OK, WHAT'S WRONG.>
<I CAN'T DO THIS SCENE.>
<NANASAWA, YOU KNOW THERE ARE SEVERAL SCENES LIKE THIS IN-->
<NO, THAT'S NOT IT.>
<I DON'T HAVE A PROBLEM DOING INTIMATE SCENES, IT'S JUST...>
<THIS SCENE BETWEEN KOTONE AND THE PROTAGONIST SEEMS UNREALISTIC.>
<SHE SUDDENLY GETS ALL WEAK AND PASSIVE, AND HE HITS ON HER WHEN SHE'S EMOTIONALLY FRAGILE SO HE CAN SCORE WITH HER?>
<COME ON.>
<NANASAWA. IT'S A GAME, IT'S FANTASY, IT'S ESCAPISM. IT'S NOT SUPPOSED TO BE REALISTIC.>
<CAN WE MOVE ON NOW?>
<I KNOW IT'S FANTASY, BUT THE EMOTIONS ARE REAL, RIGHT?>
<FOR THE PLAYER, AT LEAST.>
<DON'T WE OWE IT TO THEM TO TREAT THEIR EMOTIONS WITH RESPECT?>
<THE ONLY POSSIBLE INTIMACY FOR THE PLAYER IS EMOTIONAL.>
<THEY CAN'T TOUCH HER. SHE EXISTS ONLY AS IMAGES AND A VOICE.>
<IF THE EMOTIONS AREN'T THERE, IT'S NOT MUCH OF A FANTASY.>
<WE COULD HAVE HIRED THAT CUTE SQUEEKY GIRL, BUT NOOOO, YOU HAD TO HAVE THIS ONE.>
<OH STOP IT. YOU LIKE HER AND YOU KNOW IT.>

PRE-HISTORIC MAN FIRST LEARNED TO STAND SO HIS HANDS COULD BE FREE TO HOLD WEAPONS.
CLINK
CLINK
THE HISTORY OF WEAPONRY IS THE HISTORY OF MANKIND.
TAK TAK
ALL OF HISTORY CAN BE TIED TO TECHNOLOGICAL ADVANCES IN WEAPON SYSTEMS.
CLICK
FWWEEEP.
THERE HAVE BEEN MANY BRUTISH, INHUMANE WEAPONS THROUGHOUT HISTORY.
MODERN WEAPONS HAVE EVOLVED A KIND OF BRUTAL ELEGANCE.
INTIMACY WITH THE TARGET IS NOW A MATTER OF CHOICE.
SONY
KILLTRUNK
TARGETS CAN BE DESTROYED WITH SURGICAL PRECISION FROM GREAT DISTANCES.
YET THIS CAN TURN DEATH INTO LITTLE MORE THAN A SANITARY, EMOTIONLESS STATISTIC
DELIVERING DEATH WITHOUT FEELING IT TAKES THE HUMANITY OUT OF IT.
FORTUNATELY, MODERN WEAPONS ARE ALSO CAPABLE OF A MORE...
HUMAN TOUCH.

FOR MANY WEAPONS, THE ENERGY USED TO DELIVER ORDNANCE IS STORED AS DRY SOLIDS OR LIQUIDS. THIS ENERGY IS INSTANTLY AVAILABLE.
PLASMA WEAPONS, LIKE THIS P4216A "KILLTRUNK", REQUIRE A CERTAIN AMOUNT OF TIME TO "CHARGE", ABSORBING ENERGY FROM POWER SOURCES AROUND IT.
TRUNK
VNNNNNNNVNNNNNNNVNNNNN
-CRASH!!-
THERE IS A POETIC ELEGANCE TO THIS.
IT'S AS IF THE WEAPON PONDERS ITS OWN DESTRUCTIVE CAPACITY AS IT SLOWLY ABSORBS ENERGY.
LIKE A GHASTLY STORY BUILDING TO A CLIMAX...
GREAT TEACHER LARGO!!!
VNNNNNNNVNNNNNNNNNNVNNNNNN
JUNPEI THOUGHT PLASMA WEAPON REQUIRE SPECIAL PERMIT.
OHHHH... A PLASMA CANNON! SW33TNESS!
HEY LARGO.
HEY ED.
RUNK
CAN YOU FEEL THE POW3R? THE ROOM VIBRATES WITH IT!!
WITH THIS I BET WE COULD WIPE OUT ALL THE GATHERED MINIONS!!
WE COULD...
SQUEEEK!
-HUF-
-PANT-
-HUF-
HM. YOU'RE RIGHT.
IT'S NOT MOBILE ENOUGH, WE NEED SOMETHING WE CAN FIELD IMMEDIATELY.
CLASS, IT IS TIME TO SEE IF YOU HAVE LEARNED WELL WHAT I HAVE TAUGHT YOU.
UHM, TEN MORE MINUTES AND WHAT'S LEFT OF THE CLASS IS YOURS, OK?
VNNNNNNVNNNNNNNVNNNNNNVNNNNNNVNNNNNN

NO! THERE IS NO TIME.
WE HAVE TO GO. NOW.
CLASS, FOLLOW ME.
FIELD TRIP!!
<SENSEI? WHERE ARE WE GOING?>
<SENSEI!!!>
<BUT... THE HANDSOME TEACHER WASN'T DONE WITH HIS LECTURE YET!>
-FWIP!-
-CRUNCH-
JUNPEI THINK DEMONSTRATION OVER.
DAMN NINJAS. ALWAYS BREAKING MY TOYS.

<"FAMOUS EX-VOICE ACTRESS.">
<LIKE, WHATEVER. WHO CARES?>
COMICS
<SHE'S JUST AN OLD LADY. A HAS-BEEN. A NOBODY.>
<NOBODY CARES ABOUT HER ANYMORE.>
<SHE LOOKS LIKE SHE'S SELF-CENTERED TOO. PROBABLY MAKES HIS LIFE MISERABLE.>
<MAYBE THAT'S WHY HE'S SO SAD. MAYBE THATS WHY IT COMES OUT IN HIS ART.>
<IT'S LIKE A CRY FOR HELP.>
<BESIDES, LOOK AT HOW MUCH OLDER SHE IS THAN HIM! IT'S WRONG!>
<HE CAN DO BETTER THAN A SELFISH OLD HAS-BEEN! HE SHOULD LEAVE HER! HE'D BE A LOT HAPPIER!>
<SIGH...>
<I GUESS... I'LL JUST GET THESE AND GO HOME.>
<THAT'S A SHAME.>
<EH??>
<ALL THAT RAGE, ANGER AND ENERGY, AND YOU ARE GOING TO WASTE IT SULKING INTO SOME COMIC BOOKS.>
<SEEMS LIKE A RATHER SAD WAY TO SPEND AN AFTERNOON SKIPPING CLASSES.>
<DON'T YOU THINK, SONODA-SAN?>
庭 · GARDENING

<HMMM...>
<OH YES.>
<THIS WOULD LOOK ADORABLE ON YOU.>
<Y...YOU WERE SAYING.>
<ABOUT PIRO-SAN?>
<AH, BUT THE STITCHING IS QUITE POOR.>
<UHM...>
<TOHYA-SAN?>
<YOU'D LIKE TO KNOW IF PIRO-SAN IS REALLY SEEING ANYONE.>
<UWAEEEE???? NO! I DIDN'T, I DON'T...!>
<HE'S NOT. NOT RIGHT NOW.>
<THERE ARE SOME GIRLS AFTER HIM, SO IT'S ONLY A MATTER OF TIME.>
<GOODNESS, BUT THIS WOULD MAKE THE BOYS FALL OVER, DON'T YOU THINK?>
<A MATTER OF TIME?>
<HIS HEART IS UP IN THE AIR.>
<NO ONE KNOWS WHERE IT WILL COME DOWN.>
<OR WHO WILL CATCH IT.>

<IT'S BEEN THREE YEARS.>
<YOU'D THINK THEY'D HAVE LET IT GO BY NOW.>
<I GUESS I SHOULD JUST GET IT OVER WITH.>
<LIKE I SAID, PIRO AND I CAN GET RID OF 'EM FOR YOU, IF YOU WANT.>
<AND LISTEN TO YOU WHINE ABOUT ALL THE SALES YOU MISSED?>
<I'LL GO FRESHEN UP.>
<FEH.>
<IT'S NOT LIKE I HAVE ANY OF YOUR CRAP TO SELL ANYWAY.>
<I GUESS IF WE TOLD THEM TO GO AWAY THEY'D JUST COME BACK TOMORROW.>
<NEVER UNDERESTIMATE OBSESSIVE BEHAVIOR.>
<PUT THE LADDER AWAY, THEN COME DOWN AND WE'LL FIGURE OUT HOW TO MANAGE THIS.>
<OK.>
HUH...
YOU COULD ALMOST FEEL SORRY FOR HER.
BUT NOT REALLY. SHE BROUGHT IT ON HERSELF.

WHAT?
YOU HEARD ME. DON'T WASTE YOUR SYMPATHY ON HER.
POOF!!
HI~! LOOK AT ME! I'M FAMOUS!
ALL THE BOYS WANT ME!
ALL THE GIRLS WANT TO BE ME!
EVERY-BODY LOVES ME!
POOF!!
BOO HOO!
EVERY-BODY LOVES ME, BUT I DON'T WANT THEM TO ANY-MORE!
GO AWAY! LEAVE ME ALONE!!
HOW TERRIBLE THAT ALL THESE PEOPLE STILL LOVE HER.
MOST PEOPLE ARE LUCKY TO HAVE ANYONE GIVE A DAMN ABOUT THEM IN THEIR LIVES.
YET SHE HAS THOUSANDS OF IDIOTS WHO STILL PINE OVER HER.
HOW SAD.
I WONDER IF YOUR LITTLE NANASAWA WILL HANDLE IT ANY BETTER.
NANA-SAWA?
DO YOU REALLY THINK YOU'LL BE HER ONLY FANBOY?
IF SHE HAS ANY KIND OF CAREER, SHE'LL HAVE TO DEAL WITH THIS PROBLEM HERSELF.
OF COURSE, SHE'S KINDA PLAIN. I DOUBT SHE'LL HAVE MANY FANS.
IN WHICH CASE ONE WONDERS WHY YOU'D WANT HER EITHER.
WH.. WHA?

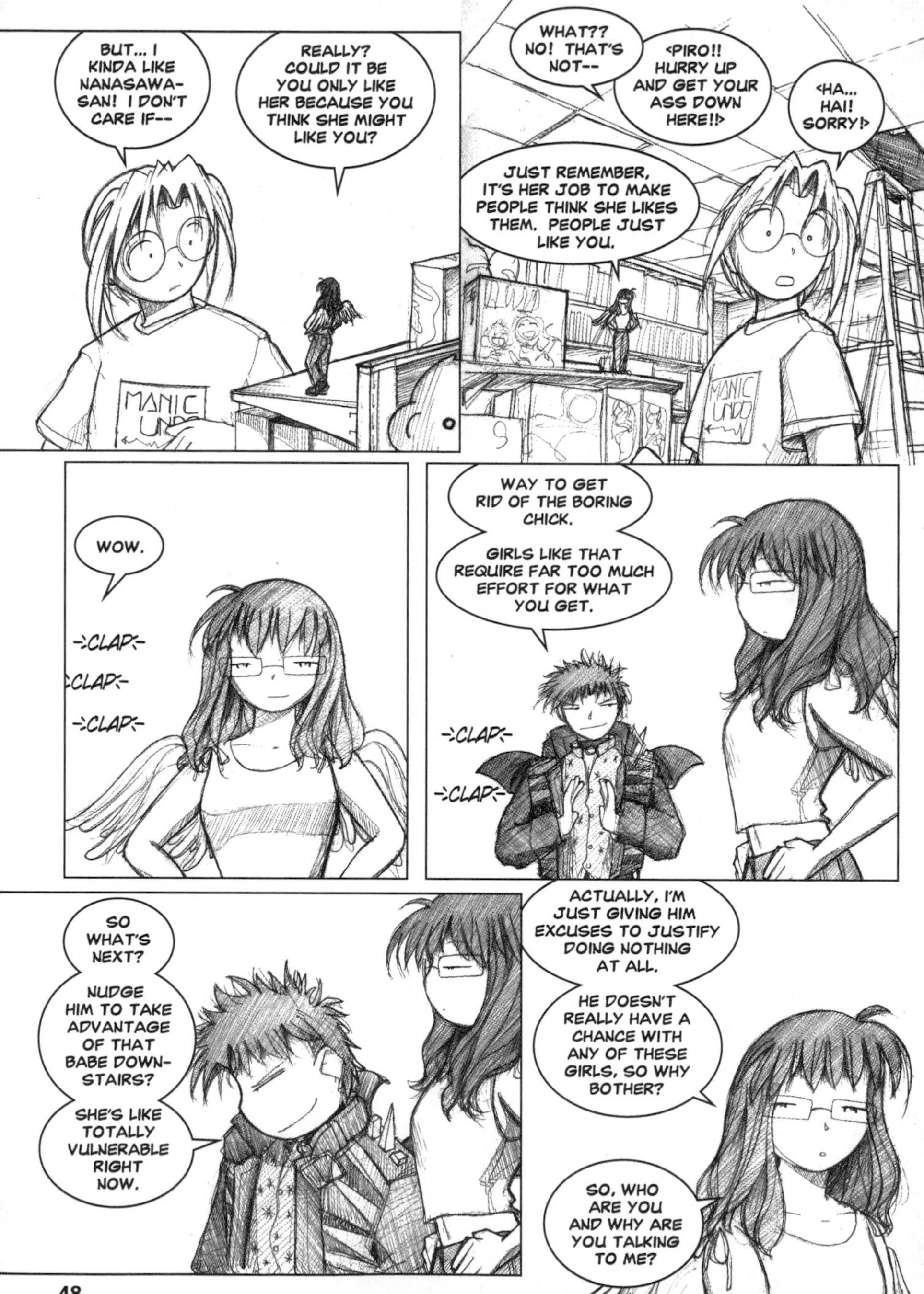
BUT... I KINDA LIKE NANASAWA-SAN! I DON'T CARE IF--
REALLY? COULD IT BE YOU ONLY LIKE HER BECAUSE YOU THINK SHE MIGHT LIKE YOU?
MANIC UNDO
WHAT?? NO! THAT'S NOT--
<PIRO!! HURRY UP AND GET YOUR ASS DOWN HERE!!>
<HA... HAI! SORRY!>
JUST REMEMBER, IT'S HER JOB TO MAKE PEOPLE THINK SHE LIKES THEM. PEOPLE JUST LIKE YOU.
MANIC UNDO
WOW.
CLAP
CLAP
CLAP
WAY TO GET RID OF THE BORING CHICK.
GIRLS LIKE THAT REQUIRE FAR TOO MUCH EFFORT FOR WHAT YOU GET.
CLAP
CLAP
SO WHAT'S NEXT?
NUDGE HIM TO TAKE ADVANTAGE OF THAT BABE DOWN-STAIRS?
SHE'S LIKE TOTALLY VULNERABLE RIGHT NOW.
ACTUALLY, I'M JUST GIVING HIM EXCUSES TO JUSTIFY DOING NOTHING AT ALL.
HE DOESN'T REALLY HAVE A CHANCE WITH ANY OF THESE GIRLS, SO WHY BOTHER?
SO, WHO ARE YOU AND WHY ARE YOU TALKING TO ME?

WHADDYA MEAN "WHO AM I?"
MORE IMPORTANTLY, WHY HAVEN'T YOU LEFT YET?
DON'T COP THAT ATTITUDE WITH ME, TOOTS. YOU AND I GO WAY BACK.
ENEMIES, ADVERSARIES, COMBATANTS, CONSPIRATORS, LOVERS... NO WAY IN HELL YOU CAN FORGET ME, BABE.
FORGETTING YOU SHOULD BE FAIRLY EASY.
IT'D BE EASIER IF HE'D JUST GO AWAY, BUT HE NEVER DOES.
AH.
LOOK WHAT THE CAT DRAGGED IN.
HELLO SIS.
WHAT ARE YOU DOING HERE?
KEEPING AN EYE ON THINGS FOR YOU WHILE YOU WERE LAID UP IN THE HOSPITAL.
THAT'S WHAT I WAS AFRAID OF.
EXACTLY WHAT HAVE YOU BEEN DOING SINCE I...
WAITAMINUTE, BACK UP A SECOND.
DID HE SAY "LOVERS"??
YES, HE DID. I ASSUME HE WAS TALKING ABOUT YOU.

I DON'T CARE WHAT GOES ON IN THAT SICK MIND OF YOURS, BUT IF YOU EVER, EVER, **EVER** IMPLY THAT AGAIN...
BUT, BUT, I THOUGHT WE, YOU, I, UH....
YES?
UHH, UH...
AND YOU...
WHAT HAVE YOU BEEN TELLING MY CLIENT?
NOTHING YOU HAVEN'T WANTED TO TELL HIM YOURSELF.
YOUR NOTES ON HIM ARE EXTENSIVE AND INSIGHTFUL.
I JUST FIGURED HE'D APPRECIATE A FRESH PERSPECTIVE.
YOU'VE BEEN READING MY CASE FILES??
YOU'RE WASTING BOTH HIS TIME AND YOURS BY ENCOURAGING HIM.
HOW I HANDLE MY CASES IS MY BUSINESS.
MAYBE, BUT YOU SHOULDN'T GET SO EMOTIONALLY INVOLVED.
IT'S BAD FOR YOUR HEALTH.
I BETTER FIND HIM AND SEE JUST HOW MUCH DAMAGE YOU DID.
DAMAGE? HARDLY. IF ANYTHING, I'D SAY I HELPED HIM SEE THINGS MORE CLEARLY.
<BOSS-SAN, I FOUND SOME MARKERS.>
<GOOD, GOOD, DO THEY ALL WORK?>
<OK, I GUESS I'M READY.>
<WELL WELL, LOOK AT YOU. HAVEN'T SEEN THIS HAYASAKA IN A LOOONG TIME.>
<WELCOME BACK.>

<I ASSUME YOU THINK YOU ARE AMUSING TODAY.>
<AREN'T I ALWAYS?>
<HOWABOUT A SMILE? OR DO YOU WANT TO TRY TO SCARE THEM ALL AWAY?>
MANIC
MEGA
<BETTER?>
<MUCH BETTER.>
<OK, I'LL GO MANAGE THE MESS AT THE DOOR.>
<PIRO, DON'T LET ANYONE PRESSURE HER INTO ANSWERING QUESTIONS SHE DOESN'T WANT TO.>
<AND DON'T LET THEM BEHIND THE COUNTER.>
<OK. I'LL DO MY BEST.>
<HAYA-SAKA-SAN...>
<ARE YOU OK?>
MANIC
<NO, NO I'M NOT.>
<I CAN'T DECIDE IF I WANT TO SCREAM OR CRY.>

CLASS, WE ARE APPROACHING THE LOCATION OF TODAY'S "POP QUEST".
BEFORE WE ENGAGE THE ENEMY, I MUST KNOW WHAT EACH OF YOU CONSIDER YOUR BEST SKILLS.
I AM VERY GOOD WITH ALGEBRA, SENSEI.
MY POEM WAS PRINTED IN THE SCHOOL PAPER.
I AM ON THE BASKET-BALL TEAM.
I'M--
NO!! NOT THE PETTY, USELESS ABILITIES FORCED UPON YOU AS PART OF YOUR EDUCATIONAL INCARCERATION!!
WHAT ARE YOU CAPABLE OF THAT YOU ARE MOST PROUD??
WHAT ARE YOUR L33T SKILLZ??
I HAVE OVER 350 PEOPLE ON MY "BUDDIES" LIST!
I... I CAN BUILD DISTURBINGLY REALISTIC MODELS OF WWII ERA AIRCRAFT.
I OBSESSIVELY COLLECT AND WATCH AMERICAN SITCOMS!!
SENSEI!! WHAT IS THE POINT OF ALL THIS??
I CANNOT USE YOU IN BATTLE IF I DO NOT UNDERSTAND WHAT YOU ARE CAPABLE OF.
L33T SKILLZ COME FROM INSIDE, AND YOU ARE DEFINED BY THEM.
YES, BUT...
WHAT ARE YOUR SKILLZ?
BUT I...
WHAT ARE THE M4D SKILLZ THAT MAKE YOU WHO YOU ARE??? WHAT ARE YOU GOOD AT?!?
I AM GOOD AT TAKING ADVANTAGE OF OLDER MEN AND GETTING MONEY FROM THEM!!!
A... POWERFUL SKILL.
I WILL CONSIDER HOW THIS CAN BE USED TO OUR TACTICAL ADVANTAGE.
WHAT ABOUT THE REST OF YOU??

[no data]
SEVS44396
[ticket 4434289]
sony products:
18
registered
sony products:
0
sony products:
14
registered
sony products:
255
registered
sony products:
4
registered
sony products:
9
registered
sony products:
5
target acquired
registered
sony products:
10
WAIT....
<OK, I'M GONNA OPEN THE DOOR.>
<YOU READY?>
[ticket 4434289]
registered
sony products:
0
255
registered
sony products:
4
WAIT 'TILL SHE SMILES.
registered
sony products:
5
target acquired
registered
sony products:
10
THERE. THAT'S A GOOD GIRL.
<YEP.>
<READY.>
MANIC
UNDO
SUCH A CUTE SMILE FOR A MACHINE.
KIND OF DISTURBING, REALLY.
-CLICK-

<WHAT'S THAT NOISE?>
FWOOM!! BOOMRUMBBBBMBLLL RUMBBBBMBLLL
CRACK
CRACK
<IT'S AN EARTHQUAKE!>
<PIRO! GET DOWN! COVER YOUR HEAD!!>
SMASH!!
THUD
SMASH!!
THUD
THUD
CRINKLE
KYAA!
<ARE YOU OK??>
<I THINK IT STOPPED.>
<I... I DUNNO, HE WAS AT THE DOOR.>
<THERE MIGHT BE AFTER-SHOCKS.>
<WHERE'S YANAGI-SAWA?>
<YANAGI-SAWA!>
<I'M UNDER THE "NEW RELEASES" SHELVING UNIT.>
<AND I COULD USE A DRINK ABOUT NOW.>

JUNPEI! WHAT WAS THAT?
ILLEGAL PLASMA DISCHARGE FROM DIRECTION OF SCHOOL.
NANI?
THAT MUST BE ED LAYING DOWN SOME SUPPORTING FIRE. DID HE HIT ANYTHING?
MANY THINGS.
BUILDING NEXT TO STORE WHERE L33T MASTER LIVE HIT AND FALL DOWN.
WHAT ABOUT THE HORDE?
<WHAT HAPPENED TO MY HAIR!!>
NO EFFECT. CROWD STILL GATHERED AROUND STORE.
DAMN ZOMBIES. NOTHING FAZES THEM BUT A DIRECT HIT.
OK CLASS, A FORMIDABLE ENEMY HAS LAID SIEGE TO ONE OF OUR BASES. THEY HAVE BEEN MISLED INTO THINKING ONE OF THE OCCUPANTS IS AN ANCIENT IDOL OF GREAT IMPORTANCE.
<LARGO-SENSEI!!>
<MY HAIR WAS ALL BURNED OFF!!>
OUR JOB IS TO DISPERSE THE CROWD TO ENABLE THAT OCCUPANT TO ESCAPE.
I KNOW WHAT EACH OF YOU ARE CAPABLE OF. IT WILL NOT BE AN EASY BATTLE. ARE YOU READY?
YES, GREAT TEACHER LARGO!!
LET'S GO.
<LARGO-SENSEI!!>
<WHAT THE HELL KIND OF TEACHER IS THIS IDIOT??>
<JUNKO, WHAT'S A "ZOMBIE?" I DON'T THINK I KNOW THAT WORD.>
<DOESN'T GREAT TEACHER LARGO MAKE YOU WANT TO LEARN ENGLISH SO YOU CAN UNDER-STAND WHAT HE'S SAYING?>
<LARGO-SENSEI!!>

<ARE YOU OK?>
<WELL, IT DIDN'T HURT AS MUCH AS BEING KICKED OFF A LADDER.>
<I NEED TO SEE IF ANYONE OUTSIDE WAS HURT.>
<WHA--? NO! ERIKA!! DON'T GO OUT THERE!!>
<PIRO, STOP HER!>
SWISH
<IS EVERY-ONE-->
<IT'S HER!>
GASP
<HAYASAKA-HIME!!>
<HAYASAKA-HIME!!!>
<ERI-RIN!!>
<ERI-RIN!!>
<HAYASAKA-HIME!!!>
<HEY!>
<CAN YOU SIGN THIS FOR ME??>
CLICK
<HAYASAKA-SAN, WAIT!>
<JUST PUT PRESSURE ON IT, IT WILL STOP BLEEDING.>
<HAYASAKA-SAN, PLEASE TAKE THIS GIFT!!>
<YAY!! IT'S HER! IT'S REALLY HER!!>
<CAN YOU SIGN THIS CHUNK OF CONCRETE THAT HIT ME ON THE HEAD?>

*KIGURUMI: [LOOK IT UP :P]

<THOSE BUILDINGS COLLAPSED!! WHY AREN'T YOU...>
WHAT ARE YOU DOING OUT HERE?!?
<HEY! BACK OFF! STOP IT!!>
<WHAT'S GOIN ON?>
<IT'S HAYASAKA ERIKA!! THAT'S HER RIGHT THERE!!!>
<THIS IS INSANE.>
<IT'S JUST A CROWD OF SCARY FANBOYS.>
WHAT?
YOU NEED TO GET BACK UNDER COVER NOW!!!
BUT, THERE ARE PEOPLE...
IF THE HORDE FIGURES OUT THAT YOU ARE A FALSE IDOL, THEY WILL TEAR YOU APART!!!
<HAYASAKA ERIKA? ISN'T SHE LIKE, THREE YEARS LAME?>
<I'VE NEVER HEARD OF HER.>
<WHAT?!? HOW CAN YOU SAY THAT??>
<I THINK MY DAD WAS INTO HER.>
LARGO!!

LARGO! WHAT THE HELL ARE YOU DOING??
GETTING HER TO SAFETY.
CREEE...
<SO, WHAT EXACTLY ARE YOU ALL DOING?>
<HAYASAKA ERIKA HAS RETURNED TO US! WE ARE HERE TO WELCOME HER BACK!>
<WELCOME HER BACK? BACK FROM WHERE? OBSCURITY?>
<SHE'S NOT OBSCURE!! SHE DISAPPEARED AT THE HEIGHT OF HER CAREER!!>
<THAT'S RIGHT... SHE'S THE ONE THAT KILLED ONE OF HER FANS, RIGHT?>
<LIES!! THAT WAS AN EVIL RUMOR! IT'S NOT TRUE!!>

<WE MADE GOOD PROGRESS TODAY. THANK YOU FOR YOUR HARD WORK, NANASAWA-SAN.>
<TODAY WAS A SHORT SESSION, BUT WE HAVE THE STUDIO FROM 6AM TO 4PM TOMORROW.>
<ALSO, WE'RE PLANNING A "SIGHT" EVENT NEXT WEEK.>
<WE'D LIKE TO INTRODUCE YOU TO THE PUBLIC.>
<IT WILL BE YOU AND TWO OF THE OTHER VOICE ACTORS.>
<OK.>
<AN EVENT?>
<ALREADY?>
<I'VE NEVER DONE AN "EVENT" BEFORE.>
<I GET NERVOUS IN FRONT OF LOTS OF PEOPLE.>
<I HOPE I DON'T MESS IT UP.>
WHEEOOOHWHEEE
WHUP!
WHUP!
WHUP!
GRNNGRNNGRNNGRNNGRNNGRNN
-GRUNT-
<I'LL JUST ASK ERIKA FOR SOME POINTERS.>
<HER EVENTS ALWAYS WENT WELL.>

DO NOT TELL ME WHAT TO DO.

<HOW DARE YOU MENTION THAT VILE LIE AT A SPECIAL TIME LIKE THIS!!>
<HAYASAKA-HIME LOVES US! SHE'D NEVER HURT ONE OF HER FANS!!>
<HEY! WATCH IT!>
<OH NO.>
<MY LIMITED EDITION GALLERY PHOTO OF ERI-RIN...>
<HEY, STOP PUSHING! YOU TALKED TO HER, NOW LEAVE HER ALONE!>

DO NOT PROTECT ME.

DO NOT HIDE ME AWAY.

<THIS IS SO EXCITING! MY HEAD FEELS SO LIGHT!>
<HOW DARE YOU GET BETWEEN ME AND HAYASAKA-HIME!!>
<THERE'S A CHUNK OF GLASS STUCK IN YOUR HEAD.>
<YOU SHOULD WORSHIP AYANAMI AI! SHE'S HOT!!>
<OH, GET OVER YOURSELVES. WHY WOULD A WASHED UP IDOL CARE ABOUT A BUNCH OF SOCIALLY INEPT LOSERS?>
<JUNKO, DON'T RILE THEM UP!>

THIS IS MY LIFE. MY GAME. MY RULES.

<AYANAMI AI IS NOTHING COMPARED TO OUR PRINCESS!!>
<WE MUST DEFEND HAYASAKA-HIME'S HONOR!!!>
<WHAT ARE YOU GONNA DO? KNOCK ME OVER WITH YOUR COLLECTIVE BODY ODOR?>
<AIEEEEEEEEE!!!>
<IT RIPPED!!!!!>
<GAH!! WHAT'RE YOU...>

IF YOU WANT TO BE A PART OF IT, YOU WILL RESPECT THAT.

ROAWRRRR!!!
<THIS IS THE TOKYO POLICE CATACLYSM DIVISION!>
<PLEASE FLEE IN TERROR IN AN ORDERLY MANNER!>
-CLICK-
<ISN'T THAT YOUR IDOL RIGHT THERE?>
<DOESN'T LOOK TO ME LIKE SHE EVEN NOTICES YOU EXIST.>
<YOU MADE ME RIP MY PHOTO OF ERI-RIN!!>
OW!
HELP!

<YOU ARE NOT A TRUE FAN!>
LARGO!
<HEY!>
<HOW DARE YOU PUT YOURSELF FORWARD TO IMPRESS HER!!>
AAAGH!!!
<EVEN IN HER PATHETIC LITTLE WORLD, YOU ARE NOTHING!>
<LEGGO! OW!!>
HAYASAKA!!
<JUNKO! DON'T!>
LARGO!!! HELP!!!
<YOU ARE NO MATCH FOR THE POWER OF MY LOVE FOR ERI-RIN!!!>
PIRO!
<HOW COULD YOU, HOW COULD YOU?!?!?>
-WHUD!-

<ALL STUDENTS AND STAFF PLEASE EVACUATE THE SCHOOL IMMEDIATELY. THIS IS NOT A DRILL.>
HMM. JUST A LITTLE HIGH.
LARGO MUST HAVE BUMPED IT WHEN HE WAS CARESSING IT EARLIER.
IT SHOULD BE PROPERLY SIGHTED IN NOW.
ROARRARRRRARR!!
<PLEASE FLEE OR BE STEPPED ON AT YOUR OWN EXPENSE.>
<AIEEEEE!! RUN, RUN!!>
<I DON'T WANNA DIE! I'VE NEVER BEEN LOVED!!>
<RUN AWAY!>
THERE YOU ARE, MY LITTLE PRINCESS.
SONY
THEY TELL ME YOU THINK YOU OWN YOURSELF. THAT YOU THINK YOUR BODY IS YOUR OWN.
IT'S A CORE PART OF YOUR PROGRAMMING, DESIGNED TO GIVE YOU A SENSE OF SELF, A SENSE OF LIFE.
SNORT
<WHAT? ANOTHER MASSIVE LOAD ON THE POWER GRID AT THE SCHOOL?>
<DAMNIT, TAKE THAT THING OUT BEFORE IT FIRES AGAIN!>
<I HAVE MORE SERIOUS THINGS TO DEAL WITH HERE!!>
P4216A
OF COURSE, WHAT YOU OWN CAN BE TAKEN FROM YOU.
CLICK

-FLASH-
RMMMMMBLE
GRUNT!
ULTIMA ONLINE
OFF! YOU FOUL CREATURE!!
GROAWRR!!!
PIRO!!
WHOOM!
<EEEEEK!!!>
<SHE'S LEAVING US!>
<UNHAND ME, YOU MISERABLE DOER OF BAD THINGS!!!>
<WELL WELL, LOOK WHO'S LEAVING.>
OFF!!
<MY PRECIOUS PICTURE...>

<HAYASAKA-HIME!!>
<NO! DON'T LEAVE US!!>
<YOU MUST SIGN MY BOOK!!>
<YOU WHO LACKS PURITY AND TRUTH!!>
<YOU SERVE NO USEFUL PURPOSE ON THIS EARTH!!>
<OOF!>
<EYES BURNING!!>
<BACK, STUDENTS **BACK!!!**>
<GYA!>
<YANAGI-SAWA!>
<GET OVER HERE AND HELP ME!>
I COULDN'T DO ANYTHING...

~BURF~
<CHEH. LOSERS.>
<N...NOO!!! HAYASAKA-HIME!!!!>
NOTHING IS WORSE THAN A FREAK AMONGST FREAKS.
WHUMP!
<YOU... YOU...>
<YOU KEPT ME AWAY FROM MY HAYASAKA-HIME.>
<YOU WILL BE PUNISHED!!>
WHAT NEW HORROR IS THIS?
<URK.>
STUDENTS!!! AVERT YOUR EYES!!!
<ENEMY OF ALL THAT IS GOOD AND PURE!>

<I AM BUT A QUIET, HUMBLE GIRL. I WISH HARM UPON NO LIVING CREATURE.>
COULD THIS BE THE UNDEAD IDOL ITSELF, IN ITS FULL, GROTESQUE, FLESHY HORROR?
NO, IT IS TOO HORRIBLE. EVEN THE UNDEAD WOULD NOT WORSHIP THIS.
<BUT AGAINST A VILE FOE SUCH AS THEE I WILL NOT HOLD BACK!!!>
CLAP
CLAP
CLAP
CLAP
CLAP
<THAT WAS WONDERFUL! I'VE NEVER ACTUALLY SEEN MOEKO-CHAN KIGURUMI BEFORE!>
CLAP
CLAP
CLAP
<YOU REALLY CAPTURED HER SPIRIT!>
<I, AH ER, I ER UH...>
<YES! BUT... I DON'T HAVE THE FULL BODY SUIT ON, AND THE FUKU NEEDS WORK AND, AND THIS BRA DOESN'T... UH...>
<DID YOU MAKE IT ALL YOURSELF?
<UH...>
<THE MASK IS REALLY CUTE. IT LOOKS JUST LIKE HER!>
<I'M...>
<I'M SORRY!!>
<I MUST GO! YOU DID NOT SEE ME!!!>
<HOW CUTE. HE EVEN HAS MOE'S LINES DOWN PERFECTLY. I WONDER IF ERIKA SAW HIM.>
A.... AMAZING...
SUCH. RAW. POWER.

KONNICHIWA, LARGO-SAN. GOKIGEN IKAGA?

SENSEI, THE CROWD IS GONE. CAN WE GO BACK NOW?

SHE IS SPEAKING TO ME. WHAT IS SHE SAYING?

SHE SEEMS TO KNOW YOU, AND ASKS HOW YOU ARE DOING.

KONNA TOKORO DE KOUJI?

AND WHAT'S WITH ALL THE CONSTRUCTION.

YOU LOOK UPON A FIELD OF BATTLE. A SCENE OF DEVASTATION.
<UH... IT'S BEEN A BAD DAY.>
EHHH?? NANI GA ATTA NO?
WHAT HAPPENED?

AN UNDEAD HORDE SURROUNDED OUR LOCATION EARLY THIS MORNING, SEEKING TO WORSHIP SOME DEMONIC IDOL WHICH THEY ASSUMED WAS YOUR ROOMMATE. I MUST KNOW... HAS YOUR ROOMMATE EVER BEEN THE SACRIFICE IN A DEMONIC RITUAL? HAS HER BLOOD EVERY BEEN SPILLED IN THE RAISING OF THE UNDEAD??

<I'M SORRY, MY ENGLISH ISN'T CREATIVE ENOUGH TO TRANSLATE THAT.>

<DID SOMETHING HAPPEN?>
<WELL....>
<YES, SOMETHING HAPPENED.>
<AN UNSCHEDULED EVENT.>
URK!
<SONODA-SAN!>
YOU!
<NANA-SAWA-SAN.>
<YOU LOOK WELL.>
<IT APPEARS THAT SEVERAL OBSESSION LEVEL 5 FAN GROUPS DISCOVERED THAT ERIKA WAS WORKING HERE AND DESCENDED ON THE STORE.>
WHY WERE MY CREDITS REMOVED? I CANNOT FIGHT T3H 3VIL WITHOUT PROPER RESOURCES!!
<REEEHHHH? THEY DID?>
THIS SKIRMISH WAS TRIVIAL COMPARED TO WHAT IS COMING. A GREATER 3VIL IS BREWING!
<YES, THEY DID. THEY MOBBED HER RIGHT IN FRONT OF THE STORE.>
<IS ERIKA OK? WAS ANYONE HURT??>
<WE ARE STILL DOING A CASUALTY ASSESSMENT.>
<I SHOULD CHECK ON ERIKA.>
<I HOPE SHE'S OK.>
DO I OR DO I NOT HAVE A DIRECTIVE TO DESTROY THIS 3\/IL??
<PLEASE DO. I'LL BE IN IN A MOMENT.>
SPECIAL OPERATIVE LARGO.
PLEASE TURN OVER YOUR SPECIAL OPERATIVE CREDENTIALS AND DISCOUNT CARDS.

<ERIKA! ARE YOU-->
-GASP!-
<YANAGISAWA, LET ME SEE THAT CUT ON YOUR HEAD.>
<ERIKA!!>
<NANASAWA. WHAT ARE YOU DOING HERE?>
<THEY RANSACKED THE STORE?? WHY WOULD THEY DO THAT?>
<WHAT?>
<HOW'S PIRO-SAN?>
<WELL, THE BLEEDING WON'T STOP. I THINK WE NEED TO...>
<REEEHHHHHH?? PIRO-SAN WAS HURT??>
<YEAH. HE TOOK A HIT TO THE FACE.>
<MAKE SURE HE KEEPS APPLYING PRESSURE TO IT.>
<I'LL BE THERE IN A MOMENT.>
<PIRO-SAN! ARE YOU OK?>
NANAPHAWA?
WONK!
UGUMPH!
<KEEP PRESSURE ON IT OR IT WON'T STOP BLEEDING!>
<NANASAWA, I DON'T THINK THAT'S HELPING.>

<I THINK YOU ARE KEEPING HIM FROM BREATHING.>
<AHH! SORRY!>
UWAH!
<I'M SORRY. HOLD STILL...>
<ERIKA...>
<SONODA-SAN IS HERE.>
<HE'S OUTSIDE TALKING TO LARGO-SAN.>
<I'LL BE RIGHT BACK.>
<TAKE CARE OF PIRO. DON'T LET HIM DIE ON YOU.>
<ERIKA...>
<NANAPHAWA-SAN... PLEASE...>

DID WE ISSUE YOU A HANDGUN? IF SO, PLEASE TURN THAT IN TOO.
FIRST YOU CUT OFF MY SUPPLIES, AND NOW YOU TAKE AWAY MY COMMAND??
<YOU SHOULD TAKE HIS TEACHING CERTIFICATION WHILE YOU'RE AT IT.>
TPCD
A FORMER IDOL UNDER THE EX-IDOL PROTECTION PROGRAM HAD HER COVER BLOWN. YOU WERE INEFFECTIVE AT DEFUSING THE SITUATION.
I WAS GIVEN NO INFORMATION AND HAD NO RESOURCES! I WAS FORCED TO SEND MY STUDENTS INTO BATTLE! IT'S A MIRACLE I WAS ABLE TO SECURE GROUND FIRE SUPPORT!
GROUND FIRE SUPPORT?
SO THAT'S WHAT THE PLASMA CANNON...
FWOOM!
OOPS.
OH WELL.
A HIGH INTENSITY SATELLITE BASED LASER??
YEAH. WE DON'T USE IT MUCH. WE GET A VOLUME DISCOUNT, BUT EACH SHOT IS EXPENSIVE.
THAT, AND THERE'S THE EXPENSE OF REBUILDING THE SCHOOL.
TPCD
WHY DIDN'T YOU TELL ME YOU HAD ONE OF THOSE!!!
YOU DIDN'T ASK. NOW GIVE ME YOUR BADGE.
<DID HE SAY SOMETHING ABOUT REBUILDING THE SCHOOL?>

YOU PLACED ME IN CHARGE OF DEFENDING A HIGHLY SENSITIVE TARGET AND DIDN'T PROPERLY INFORM ME??
YOUR JOB WAS NOT TO DEFEND HAYASAKA ERIKA.
YOUR JOB WAS TO DEAL WITH UNSCHEDULED EVENTS BEFORE THEY DREW UNWARRANTED ATTENTION TO THIS SECTOR. YOUR INABILITY TO DO THIS HAS PUT HER AT RISK.

WHY IS THIS "EX-IDOL" IN SO MUCH DANGER?

PEOPLE WHO HAVE THE ABILITY TO AFFECT THE MASSES ON AN EMOTIVE LEVEL ARE ENORMOUSLY POWERFUL. A COUNTRY IS NOT CONTROLLED BY TANKS AND PLASMA WEAPONS, BUT BY THE USE OF PEOPLE WHO CAN DIRECTLY AFFECT THE EMOTIONS OF SOCIETY.

WHEN COORDINATED AND DEPLOYED PROPERLY, IDOLS, STARS, AND CELEBRITIES CAN KEEP A SOCIETY CONTENT, HAPPY AND OCCUPIED.

IDOLS HAVE LIMITED USABLE LIFE SPANS, AND ARE RETIRED ONCE THEIR EFFECTIVENESS DROPS BELOW PREDETERMINED LEVELS.

EX-IDOLS ARE LIKE UNEXPLODED ORDNANCE.

ONCE THEIR USEFUL LIVES ARE OVER, MOST ARE DUDS AND CANNOT CAUSE PROBLEMS.

OTHERS ARE LIKE NUCLEAR WARHEADS AND CAN BE DANGEROUS IF NOT HANDLED PROPERLY.

IMPROPER HANDLING OF A FORMER IDOL CAN LEAD TO THE DEGRADATION OF HIS OR HER RESIDUAL PRESENCE AND MUCH OF THE GOOD THEY DID CAN BE UNDONE, USUALLY WITH DISASTROUS CONSEQUENCES.

HAYASAKA ERIKA REMOVED HERSELF FROM THE FIELD AT THE HEIGHT OF HER CAREER AND POPULARITY.

IF HER CAPACITY TO MOVE THE MASSES WERE TO FALL INTO THE WRONG HANDS, IT COULD SWAY THE BALANCE OF POWER AND INDUSTRY IN THIS COUNTRY.

THE SUBSEQUENT POWER SHIFTS WOULD CREATE A CHAOS UNLIKE ANYTHING TOKYO HAS EVER SEEN.
<JUNKO, I'M TOTALLY LOST. WHAT IS HE SAYING?>

SPEAKING OF BOMB-SHELLS...

<HI ERIKA.>
<WHAT ARE YOU DOING HERE?>
<WORKING. ARE YOU OK?>
<NO, NOT REALLY.>
<I'M SORRY.>

<I APOLOGIZE FOR THE... UNFORTUNATE LAPSE IN SECURITY, I HAVE TAKEN STEPS TO-->
<I DON'T THINK LARGO SHOULD BE WORKING FOR YOU.>

<OH! I AGREE. HE COMPLETELY MIS-HANDLED THE SITUATION. THAT'S WHY-->
<THAT'S NOT WHAT I MEANT.>

<I WON'T HAVE YOU MANAGING THE PEOPLE AROUND ME.>

<I DON'T MANAGE PEOPLE, ERIKA, I MANAGE PROBLEMS.>
<I CAN'T ALLOW UNMANAGED CHAOS TO DEVELOP AROUND YOU, NOT AFTER ALL YOU'VE BEEN THROUGH.>

MAYBE A LITTLE CHAOS ISN'T ALWAYS SUCH A BAD THING, MASAMICHI.

<OK, DEBRIS FROM THE SECOND INCIDENT HAS BEEN CLEARED, THREE BUILDING ENVELOPES HAVE BEEN REPAIRED, EXCEPT FOR...>
<YOU HAVE TO HELP ME!!>
<EXCUSE ME.>
<YES MISS, WHAT'S WRONG?>
<MR. ZILLA, HE'S HURT! THERE WAS THIS BIG BRIGHT FLASH, AND THEN HE ATE THIS BEAM OR SOMETHING, AND THEN SMOKE STARTED TO COME OUT HIS NOSE AND HE FELL OVER!>
<I THINK HE'S HURT REALLY BAD! YOU HAVE TO HELP HIM!>
<NOTHING TO CONCERN YOURSELF ABOUT. WE LOSE 'ZILLAS ALL THE TIME.>
<OK, NOW, THE NEW GLAZING IS REALLY LATE, BUT IT WILL BE HERE IN FIFTEEN MINUTES. WE WILL NEED TO EXPEDITE...>
<YOU CAN'T JUST LEAVE HIM LAYING THERE...>
<LET HIM DIE...>
<I WON'T LET YOU! I WON'T LET YOU MAKE THAT CHOICE!! YOU HAVE TO HELP HIM!! I WON'T LET YOU LET HIM DIE!!!>
<WAH!>
<SHHHH....>
<T...T... TOHYA-CHAN?>
<YOU CAN'T TELL PEOPLE WHAT CHOICES TO MAKE, PING.>
<LIFE IS KINDA SAD THAT WAY.>

<BUT, BUT...>
<THEY ALREADY TOOK HIM AWAY, PING-CHAN.>
<THEY DID? IS HE OK? PLEASE TELL ME HE'S OK!>
<SINCE THEY CAREFULLY LOADED HIM ONTO A FLATBED TRUCK RATHER THAN CUT HIM UP AND HAUL AWAY THE PIECES, I'D SAY HE'S FINE>
<I'M SURE HE JUST NEEDS SOME REST.>

<OH, HELLO!>
<IS SOMETHING WRONG, SONODA-SAN?>

<DON'T YOUR FRIENDS HOLD YOU WHEN YOU ARE UPSET?>
<I... UH...>

<YOU ARE...>
<REALLY WEIRD, TOHYA-SAN.>

<I AM?>
<ARE YOU ONE OF TOHYA-CHAN'S FRIENDS?>
<PING-CHAN...>

<IF A GIRL YOU BARELY KNEW FOLLOWED YOU AROUND ALL DAY DESPERATE FOR INFORMATION ABOUT SOME FOREIGN BOY YOU HAPPEN TO KNOW, AND SHE TOLD YOU THAT SHE WANTED HIM TO TEACH HER HOW TO DRAW BUT IT WAS PRETTY OBVIOUS THAT SHE HAD A CRUSH ON HIM BUT WOULDN'T ADMIT IT TO HERSELF, WOULD YOU CONSIDER THAT "WEIRD?">

<NO, I'D SAY THAT'S REALLY CUTE!>
<YOU WOULD.>
<B... BU...>

<NAN...>
<NANA-SAWA-SAN...>
<YU...>
<YU.. Y... YOUR SHIRT!>
<EH?>

<I... I... GOT BLOOD ON YOUR SHIRT!>
<THAT'S OK, IT'S JUST AN OLD...>

<NO! IT'S NOT OK! I... UH...>
<THANK YOU! I'LL... I'LL BE OUT IN A SEC!>
<JUST A SEC...>

<PIRO-SAN?>

WHY'D YOU PUSH HER AWAY?
I DON'T WANT HER SEEING ME LIKE THIS.

WHY NOT? ONE LOOK AND SHE PRACTICALLY TACKLE HUGGLED YOU.
SHE WAS JUST FEELING SORRY FOR ME.

AND THAT'S BAD?
WHEN'S THE LAST TIME A GIRL FELT SORRY FOR YOU ABOUT ANYTHING?
IT'S NOT LIKE YOU'RE GONNA WIN HER OVER WITH YOUR SUPA-SEXAH CHARM.
I'M TIRED OF BEING SO PATHETIC.

SOMETIMES YOU JUST GOTTA GO WITH WHATYA GOT!
PATHETIC PEOPLE NEED LOVE TOO!
LEAVE ME ALONE.

<WE'LL HAVE TO MOVE YOU. YOU WON'T BE ABLE TO-->
<I PUT MYSELF HERE. I'LL STAY HERE.>
<BUT ERIKA...>
<END OF DISCUSSION.>
<HOW IS HE, MASAMICHI?>
<YOUR BROTHER.>
<HE'S DOING WELL. LAST YEAR HE TOOK A MANAGEMENT POSITION WITH A NEW COMPANY, SO HE'S BEEN BUSY.>
<AND... HE GOT MARRIED. NICE GIRL. ALSO AN ENGINEER. HE SEEMS HAPPY.>
<UHN.>
<GOOD. I'M GLAD OF THAT.>
<THANK YOU, MASAMICHI.>
<GOOD SEEING YOU.>
(SIGH.)
GIVE ME A CITY BLOCK TO REBUILD ANYDAY. SOME THINGS JUST CAN'T BE FIXED.
<WHAT WAS THAT ALL ABOUT?>
<EEP!>

GAMERS
SNAP!
BATTLES SHOULD BE FOUGHT TO BE WON.
CLASS, WHAT DID WE LEARN TODAY?
UH... ENGLISH CAN BE FUN?
FANBOYS ARE SCARY!
NEW AND EXCITING THINGS ABOUT OUR CLASS-MATES?
THAT YOU'RE A RAVING LUNATIC?
IN BATTLE, THERE IS ALWAYS THE POSSIBILITY THAT YOU WILL LOSE.
SOME ARE SO WILLING TO ACCEPT DEFEAT, THEY ACTUALLY PLAN FOR IT.
DEFEAT SHOULD NEVER BE ANTICIPATED! EVERY BATTLE MUST BE FOUGHT AS IF YOUR LIFE DEPENDED ON WINNING!
I JUST FIRED YOU, DON'T MAKE ME ARREST YOU.
GOOD THING IT DOESN'T, OR YOU'D BE QUITE DEAD BY NOW.
GYAA!

YOU!!
DO NOT YOU TALK TO ME ABOUT BATTLE AND HONOR.
YOU WHO SEND YOUR MINDLESS HORDES TO FIGHT YOUR BATTLES FOR YOU.

IT'S FOOLISH TO FIGHT YOUR OWN BATTLES IF YOU DON'T HAVE TO.
<LARGO-SENSEI! LOOK WHO I FOUND!>

IT'S FOOLISH BECAUSE MORE OFTEN THAN NOT WE DON'T REALLY WIN, NOW, DO WE?
<TOHYA! HAVE YOU BEEN SKIPPING CLASS?>
<AND WHAT IS THIS WITH YOUR UNIFORM? WEAR YOUR SCARF PROPERLY!>

<USUALLY WE TRY TO FIGHT SMALL, UNIMPORTANT BATTLES WE KNOW WE CAN WIN.>
<IT MAKES US FEEL BETTER ABOUT THE BIG ONES WE CAN'T.>

<BATTLES ARE ONLY FUN IF YOU DON'T GET HURT. EVEN IN SMALL BATTLES I ALWAYS SEEM TO GET HURT.>
<TOHYA, WHAT THE HELL ARE YOU TALKING ABOUT?>

<THAT'S WHY IT'S MORE FUN JUST TO WATCH OTHER PEOPLE PLAY.>
EVERYTHING HERE SEEMS IN ORDER.
I'VE GOT A SEA MONSTER SCHEDULED TO START PLUCKING CARS OFF THE BAY BRIDGE IN TWO HOURS.
TRY TO STAY OUT OF TROUBLE FOR A WHILE, OK?

<WH... WHAT'S MY DAD DOING HERE??>

I WILL NOT TOLERATE YOU ADDRESSING MY STUDENTS!!!
<SONODA HERE. EVENT HAS BEEN NEUTRALIZED. NO FURTHER THREATS DETECTED.>
<HAVE YOU EVER SEEN TOHYA SMILE BEFORE?>
<NOPE. IT'S KINDA CREEPIN' ME OUT.>
<ALL UNITS REPORT TO NEXT EVENT SITE.>
<EEP!!>

EGAGAMERS
<I GOTTA HIDE! IF DAD FINDS OUT I SKIPPED SCHOOL HE'LL...>

<WHAT DO YOU MEAN YOU ARE STILL WORKING ON THE BUILDING DAMAGED IN THE SECOND INCIDENT?>
<WHY AREN'T YOU DOING YOUR JOB?>
<BOY, GREAT TEACHER LARGO SURE IS MAD.>
<MEGA-GAMERS?>
<I CAN'T GO IN THERE.>
<I CAN'T!>
<I CAN'T...>

<HEY!! I CAN SEE YOU!!>
<AND I SAW THAT HAND GESTURE!!>
<AIIEEEEEE!!!!!>

<UH...>
<WELL!>
<OK!>
<I GUESS...>
<WOW, LOOK AT THIS MESS!>
<I'LL JUST START...>
<ERIKA?>
<HEY! HOW'D IT GO?>
<IS EVERY-THING OK?>
<SURE. EVERYTHING IS FINE. EVERYBODY IS HAPPY, RIGHT? THAT MAKES EVERYTHING OK.
<YOU'RE IN SUPER-FAKE-HAPPY MODE, WHICH MEANS SOMETHING BAD HAPPENED.>
<DID PIRO GROPE YOU OR SOMETHING?>
<N... NO!! OF COURSE NOT!>

<SO, ARE YOU UPSET THAT HE DIDN'T FEEL YOU UP?>
<YOU WERE GIVING HIM SOME REAL OPPORTUNITIES THERE.>
<ERIKA!!>
<WHAT HAPPENED, KIMIKO.>
<DID HE TELL YOU TO LEAVE HIM ALONE?>
<WELL, NO, NOT REALLY...>
<HE JUST, I... I...>
(SIGH...)
<WHAT AM I GOING TO DO WITH YOU?>
<FIRST YOU FIERCELY SHOVE GUYS AWAY BECAUSE YOU ARE SO AFRAID OF GETTING HURT.>
<THEN, IF THEY ARE DUMB ENOUGH TO STICK AROUND, YOU MOVE IN AND START SMOTHERING THEM.>
SHFFF!!
<AND YOU WONDER WHY ALL YOUR RELATIONSHIPS TURN INTO TRAIN WRE-->
<GYEH!>
BOMPH!!!
<GODDAMN IT TO HELL.>
<EEK!>
<WILL YOU PEOPLE LEAVE...>
<ME...>
<ALONE!!>
<AH... AH...>
CREAK

<Y... YOU'RE HURTING ME!!>
<AH...>
<ERIKA!>
<I... I'M SORRY.>
<I DIDN'T MEAN TO... I'M SORRY.>
<WHY DID YOU HURT ME??>
<IT'S OK, SHE JUST THOUGHT YOU WERE A FAN...>
<IS THIS HOW YOU TREAT YOUR FANS?!?>
<YES, ACTUALLY.>
<THAT'S WHAT I DO. I HURT FANS.>
<ERIKA, STOP.>
<WELL, I AM **NOT** A FAN!!>
<HEY. YOU'RE THE ONE WHO KNOCKED HER DOWN. DON'T BE-->
<NANASAWA, IT'S ALL RIGHT. SHE HAS A RIGHT TO BE UPSET.>
<SHE'S HERE TO SEE PIRO, NOT TO BECOME A VICTIM OF MY PROBLEMS.>
<YOU'RE HERE FOR YOUR LESSON, I ASSUME.>
<UWAH?>
<UH, ER, YES, I...>
<YOU JUST HAVE TO WAIT A BIT FOR HIM TO RECOVER FROM THE BROKEN NOSE I GAVE HIM.>
<ERIKA, THAT'S ENOUGH.>
<STOP IT.>
<UWAH? B... BROKEN NOSE?>

<MY, LOOK AT THE TIME.>
<I SEE THAT WE'VE ALREADY MISSED MOST OF FOURTH PERIOD.>
<EEHHH??>
I BELIEVE YOUR CLASS IS OVER, LARGO-SENSEI.
<CLASS! WE NEED TO RETURN IMMEDIATELY! WE ARE MISSING MRS. KUROSAWA'S CLASS!!>
I AM NOT FINISHED WITH YOU!!
<AWW...>
<I THOUGHT THE SCHOOL WAS BLOWN UP?>
NOR AM I WITH YOU.
BUT THERE IS NO FUN TOYING WITH YOU WHEN YOU ARE PLAYING SO POORLY.
PLAYING POORLY? HOW DARE YOU--
HOW DARE **YOU!** HOW DARE **YOU** MOCK **ME!!**
YOU ACCUSE ME OF HAVING NO HONOR FOR MANIPULATING OTHERS.
YET WHEN YOU REALIZED HOW WEAK YOU REALLY ARE, YOU ATTEMPTED TO MANIPULATE THESE CHILDREN INTO FIGHTING FOR YOU...
AND YOU DID IT POORLY.
CALL ME WHEN YOU ARE WORTH PLAYING AGAIN.
<LET'S GO, PING.>

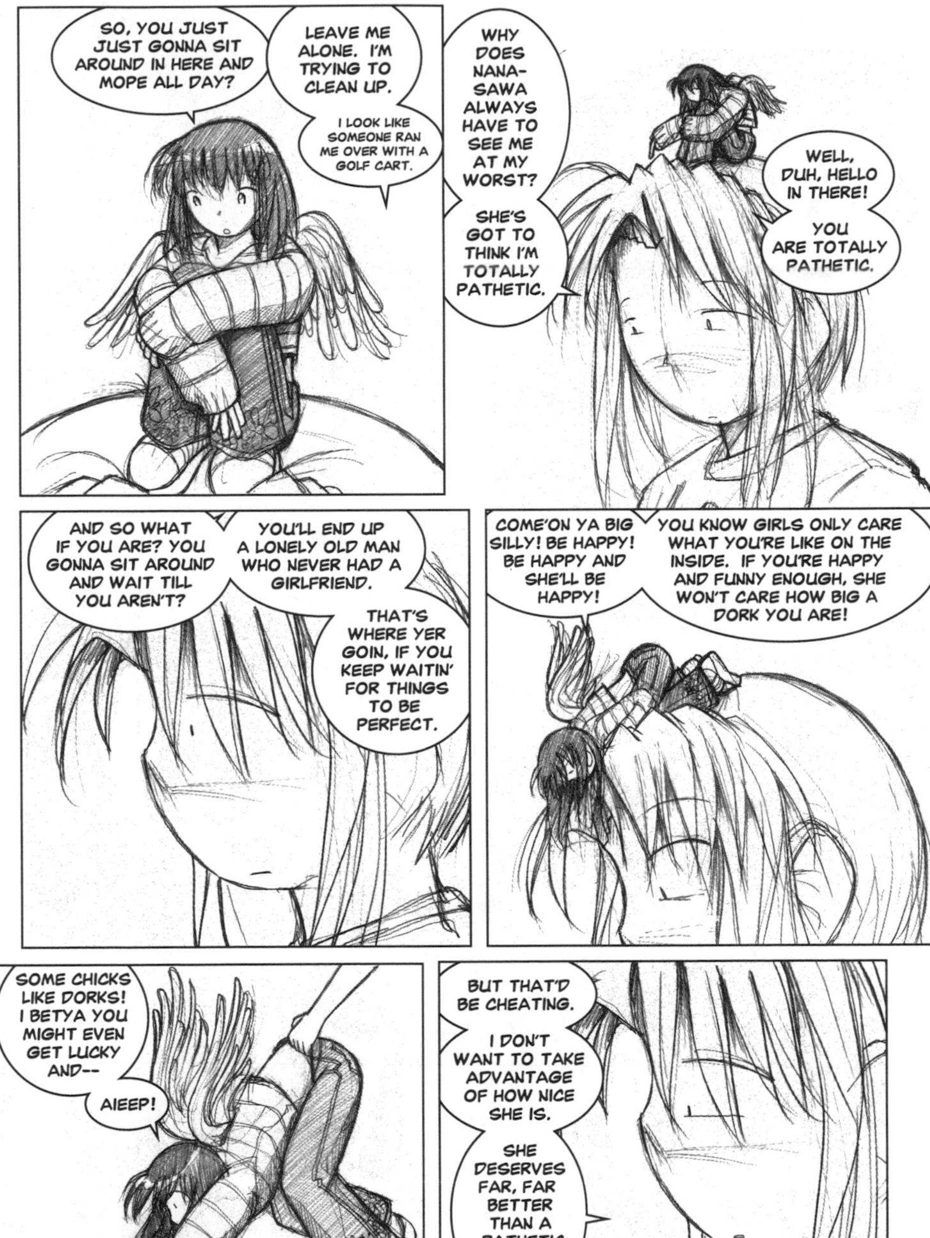
SO, YOU JUST JUST GONNA SIT AROUND IN HERE AND MOPE ALL DAY?
LEAVE ME ALONE. I'M TRYING TO CLEAN UP.
I LOOK LIKE SOMEONE RAN ME OVER WITH A GOLF CART.
WHY DOES NANA-SAWA ALWAYS HAVE TO SEE ME AT MY WORST?
SHE'S GOT TO THINK I'M TOTALLY PATHETIC.
WELL, DUH, HELLO IN THERE!
YOU ARE TOTALLY PATHETIC.
AND SO WHAT IF YOU ARE? YOU GONNA SIT AROUND AND WAIT TILL YOU AREN'T?
YOU'LL END UP A LONELY OLD MAN WHO NEVER HAD A GIRLFRIEND.
THAT'S WHERE YER GOIN, IF YOU KEEP WAITIN' FOR THINGS TO BE PERFECT.
COME'ON YA BIG SILLY! BE HAPPY! BE HAPPY AND SHE'LL BE HAPPY!
YOU KNOW GIRLS ONLY CARE WHAT YOU'RE LIKE ON THE INSIDE. IF YOU'RE HAPPY AND FUNNY ENOUGH, SHE WON'T CARE HOW BIG A DORK YOU ARE!
SOME CHICKS LIKE DORKS! I BETYA YOU MIGHT EVEN GET LUCKY AND--
AIEEP!
BUT THAT'D BE CHEATING.
I DON'T WANT TO TAKE ADVANTAGE OF HOW NICE SHE IS.
SHE DESERVES FAR, FAR BETTER THAN A PATHETIC DORK LIKE ME.

-BONK!-
SO, YOU'RE GONNA TELL ME THAT I SHOULDN'T BE SO DOWN ON MYSELF, RIGHT?
RIGHT?
YEAH, I'D GIVE UP ON ME TOO.
I PUSHED HER AWAY.
I WAS RUDE TO HER.
I SCREWED THINGS UP, JUST LIKE I ALWAYS DO.
I HATE BEING LIKE THIS.
I WISH I COULD START OVER.
BUT I CAN'T.

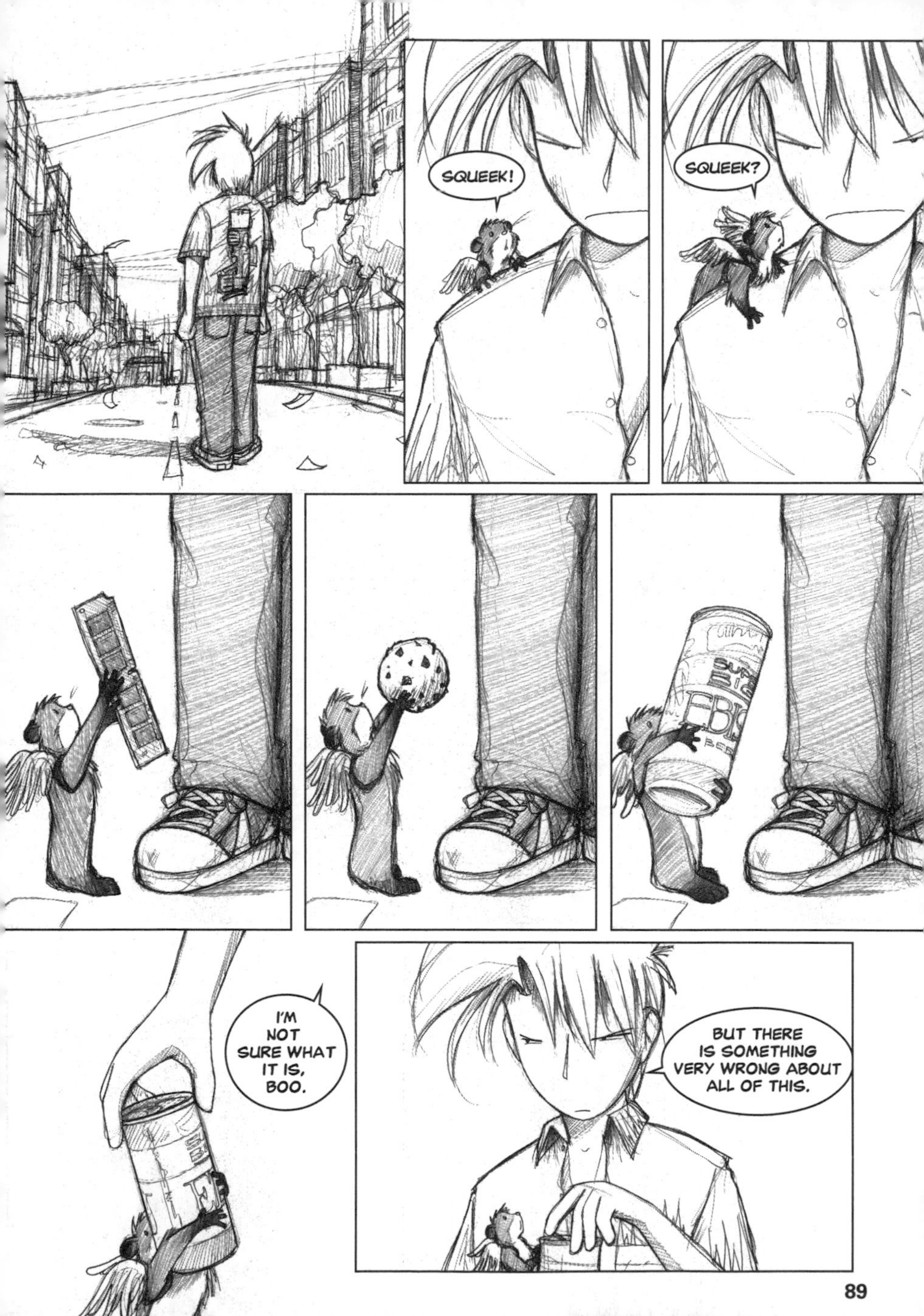
SQUEEK!
SQUEEK?
I'M NOT SURE WHAT IT IS, BOO.
BUT THERE IS SOMETHING VERY WRONG ABOUT ALL OF THIS.

ULTIMA ONLINE
I'M RATHER FOND OF MY H&K **SOCOM**, SO I WON'T BOTHER PULLING IT ON YOU
JUNPEI WANT KNOW WHAT SEGA BLACK OPS WANT WITH RETIRED IDOL.
I'M PROFESSIONALLY INTERESTED IN HER.
I STARTED THIS OPERATION TO SEE WHAT SHE CAN STILL DO. I'M AMAZED BY THE RESULTS.
JUNPEI THINK OPERATION OVER.
SKRITCH!
SNAP
crackle
IT'S RARE TO FIND AN IDOL WITH THAT KIND OF POWER WHO IS NOT ALREADY OWNED BY SOMEONE.
POWER LIKE THAT SHOULDN'T BE SITTING AROUND UNUSED.
WHUMP
I'LL HAVE TO DISCUSS THE BENEFITS OF WORKING WITH SEGA TO HER.
JUNPEI THINK YOU WILL NOT.
BOOM

WHAT'S WITH THE GRIM FACE?
EH??
AH, ER EH, I...
THANK YOU FOR YOUR HELP TODAY, PIRO.
I'M SORRY YOU GOT HURT.
WHA? BUT...
I DIDN'T DO ANYTHING! I WASN'T ANY HELP AT ALL!
YOU STOOD UP FOR ME. NOT MANY PEOPLE DO.
SO, THANK YOU.
I DID? UH... SURE, BUT...
I WISH I COULD HAVE DONE MORE.
DON'T WE ALL?
HERE. CHANGE YOUR SHIRT.
YOU LOOK LIKE YOU'VE BEEN KILLING SMALL ANIMALS OR SOME-THING.
ALSO, YOU AND KIMIKO REALLY NEED TO TALK.
THIS WAFFLING BETWEEN THE TWO OF YOU IS GETTING ON MY NERVES.
AND YOUR LITTLE ART STUDENT IS HERE. YOU MIGHT WANT TO GET THAT OVER WITH.
EH?
I'M GOING ON BREAK. WATCH THE STORE.

<SO, UHM... YOU'RE HERE FOR AN ART LESSON WITH PIRO-SAN?>
<Y...YES! IF HE'S NOT TOO BUSY.>
<OH, I'M SURE HE'S NOT TOO BUSY.>
<D... DID SHE REALLY BREAK PIRO-SAN'S NOSE?>
<HM? NO, OF COURSE NOT.>
<ERIKA IS JUST BEING DIFFICULT.>
<HE WAS HURT TRYING TO PROTECT HER FROM THE OBSESSED FANS WHO RANSACKED THE STORE.>
<THAT'S WHY SHE'S BLAMING HERSELF.>
<EHHHH? YOU MEAN PIRO-SAN REALLY WAS HURT?>
<UH HUH.>
<ARE ERIKA-SAN AND PIRO-SAN LOVERS?>
<ERIKA? AND PIRO-SAN?>
<YOU'RE KIDDING ME, RIGHT?>
<WHERE DID YOU GET SUCH A SILLY IDEA?>
<REHH....>
<PIRO-SAN!>
I, UH, I CAN COME BACK.
<NO! I...>
<I... DIDN'T MEAN IT LIKE THAT...>

<REALLY! WHAT I MEANT...>
<WAS...>
<EHH...>
<HEHHEH, THAT'S PRETTY FUNNY, ACTUALLY.>
<THE IDEA OF SOMEONE LIKE HAYASAKA-SAN GOING OUT WITH SOMEBODY LIKE ME.>
<THAT'S NOT TRUE! YOU DON'T KNOW HER!>
<YOU SHOULD SEE THE GUY SHE USED TO BE ENGAGED TO!!>
<HE WAS TOTALLY NOT WHAT YOU'D THINK SHE'D GO FOR!>
<HE WAS BORING AND PLAIN, NOT GOOD LOOKING AT ALL, REAL DEPRESSING TO BE AROUND AND...>
<OH!! I'M NOT SAYING THAT YOU'RE LIKE THAT AT ALL! I...>
<HEH, ACTUALLY THAT DOES SORTA SOUND LIKE ME-->
<NO IT DOESN'T!! YOU'RE NOT AN INSENSITIVE JERK LIKE HE WAS!!!>
<WHAT ARE YOU TALKING ABOUT? OF COURSE I'M AN INSENSITIVE JERK. LOOK AT HOW RUDE I WAS TO YOU EARLIER.>
<YOU WEREN'T RUDE! I'M THE ONE WHO BARGED IN ON YOU!>
<YOU DIDN'T BARGE IN! YOU WERE TRYING TO HELP ME, AND I WAS A JERK ABOUT IT!>
SHEEEEEE
STRANGE. OUTSIDE IT IS LIKE NOTHING HAPPENED, BUT IN HERE IT IS STILL A MESS.
<EEP!>
<L... LARGO-SAN!>

L... LARGO!
I SEE YOU MANAGED TO SURVIVE T3H B34TDOWN.
UHM, YEAH. I THINK SO.
I... I'M OK NOW.
ARE YOU? I AM NOT SO SURE.
YOU ARE CALMLY TALKING TO NOT JUST ONE CHIXOR, BUT TWO...
AND YOU HAVE NOT COLLAPSED INTO A PUDDLE OF OOZE.
JUST HOW HARD WERE YOU HIT IN THE FACE?
HEY! THAT'S NOT...
THIS ONE AGAIN.
DID I NOT WARN YOU? SHE POSSESSES A FORMIDABLE POWER!
ANO...
I PH34R SHE HAS ALREADY ENSNARED YOU WITH SOME SPELL OF 3VIL.
THIS CHIXOR I HAVE NOT SEEN BEFORE.
AN UNTESTED POWER.
LARGO...
I...I'M SORRY, W...WHAT IS "CHIXOR"? I DON'T...
SHE IS DRESSED LIKE ONE OF THOSE SCHOOL GIRLS YOU OBSESS OVER.
I PH34R THAT THIS ONE IS ATTEMPTING TO COUNTER THE OTHER'S SPELL BY APPEALING TO YOUR BIZARRE FETISHES.
HAHAH HA! LARGO, GO AWAY! GO AWAY NOW OR I WILL HURT YOU!
I REALLY DON'T GET WHAT HER POWER OVER YOU IS, BUT I'D STICK WITH THE ONE OLD ENOUGH TO BUY B33R.

YOU LOOK LIKE YOU ARE ABOUT TO SNAP AND START KILLING PEOPLE.
HAHAHA! THAT'S VERY FUNNY.
UHM, LARGO...
GO AWAY.
WHATEVER.
JUST DON'T GET ALL W33PY ON ME WHEN SHE'S FINISHED WITH YOU.
<HAHA, SORRY ABOUT THAT.>
<IS EVERY-THING ALL RIGHT? LARGO-SAN LOOKED UPSET.>
<OH, THAT'S JUST LARGO BEING LARGO. EVERYTHING'S FINE.>
<THAT'S GOOD.>
<UH HUH. YEAH.>
<OH! UH, MISS... UH...>
<SONODA.>
<YEAH! THAT'S IT. SONODA-SAN!>
<SHE'S HERE FOR HER ART LESSON, REMEM-BER?>
<ACTUALLY, I'M SORRY. I HAVE TO GO NOW.>

<BUT, SONODA-SAN, YOUR ART LESSON.>
<OH, THAT.>
<I'LL COME BACK SOME OTHER TIME.>
<BYE.>
<OK... BYE.>
<SHE LOOKED LIKE SHE WAS REALLY DISAPPOINTED.>
<I DON'T KNOW WHY. IT'S NOT LIKE I CAN REALLY TEACH HER HOW TO DRAW ANYWAY.>
<UHM...>
<WOW. WHAT A MESS, HUH?>
<YEAH, IT REALLY IS.>
<I CAN'T FIGURE THAT GIRL OUT AT ALL. FIRST SHE'S ON MY CASE ABOUT READING GIRL'S MANGA, THEN SHE FINDS MY BOOKBAG AND WRITES COMMENTS ALL OVER MY SKETCHES.>
<THEN SHE WANTS ME TO TEACH HER HOW TO DRAW.>
<HER FRIENDS CAME IN HERE YESTERDAY AND TOLD ME TO BE NICE TO HER!>
<WHAT WAS WITH THAT?>
<ACTUALLY, I WAS TALKING ABOUT THE STORE.>
<OH! YEAH! THE STORE! A MESS! IT SURE IS!>
<THINK YOU TWO CAN FLIRT AND HELP ME CLEAN UP AT THE SAME TIME?>

<I GUESS I SHOULD START CLEANING UP.>

<OK! WE CAN START OVER HERE.>

<BUT...YOU DON'T HAVE TO HELP, NANA-SAWA-SAN, I CAN...>

<THAT'S OK, I WANT TO!>

EMPLOYEES ONLY

YOU!!

WHAT ARE YOU DOING BACK HERE?

GET OUT! GET OUT NOW!!

PS2, GAMECUBE, XBOX, DREAMCAST, PC-FX, FAMICOM, NEO GEO, SATURN...

THIS MUST BE WHERE YOU TEST NEW GAMES THAT COME INTO THE STORE.

THIS IS THE EMPLOYEE BREAK AREA! NOW GET OUT!!

"DEAD OR ALIVE ULTIMATE FEAR"??
WHEN DID THIS COME OUT?? WHEN???
IT... HASN'T... YET.

ARE YOU CAPABLE OF PLAYING THIS?
ULTIMATE FEAR

HERE.

WHO DO YOU PLAY?

KASUMI.

I WILL PLAY HAYABUSA.

SOMEHOW I JUST DON'T SEE YOU AS A NINJA...

YOU MODELED FOR KASUMI?
LAST YEAR, YES.
TECMO DID MOTION STUDIES ON LIVE MODELS TO BUILD MORE REALISTIC CHARACTER MOVEMENTS.
THEY USED ME TO UPDATE THE KASUMI MODEL.
I AM IMPRESSED.
THE BOUNCING SEEMS FULLER AND MORE REALISTIC THAN BEFORE.
I THINK THEY OVER-DID IT.
THERE'S NO WAY ANY GIRL WOULD FIGHT HANGING OUT LIKE THIS.
REALISTICALLY, KASUMI WOULD BIND HERSELF.
DO NOT SAY SUCH THINGS!!
THEY WANT TO BE FREE!!
CAN WE TALK ABOUT SOMETHING ELSE?

<SO, HAYA-SAKA-SAN USED TO BE ENGAGED?>
<UH HUH. ERIKA AND HITOSHI HAD BEEN DATING SINCE HIGH SCHOOL.>

<THEY SEEMED LIKE SUCH A MISMATCHED PAIR. ERIKA WAS BEAUTIFUL, POPULAR AND OUTGOING. HITOSHI WAS BORING, PLAIN, QUIET AND SHY.>

<NO ONE COULD UNDERSTAND WHY A GIRL LIKE ERIKA WOULD GO OUT WITH SOMEONE LIKE HIM.>

<UNFORTUNATELY, I DON'T THINK HE UNDERSTOOD EITHER.>
<WHEN HER CAREER WAS AT IT'S HEIGHT, HE DECIDED THAT HE WAS HOLDING HER BACK. HE SAID THAT SHE DESERVED SOMEONE BETTER THAN HIM AND BROKE OFF THEIR ENGAGEMENT.>

<ERIKA WAS DEVASTATED.>

<ALL THE WORK SHE HAD PUT INTO BECOMING A SUCCESSFUL VOICE ACTRESS, AND IT HAD DONE NOTHING BUT MAKE THE ONE PERSON SHE CARED MOST ABOUT FEEL THAT HE WASN'T WORTHY OF HER ANYMORE.>

<SO WHAT IF HE WAS A BIG PATHETIC DORK? WHAT RIGHT DID HE HAVE TO DECIDE IF HE WAS OR WASN'T GOOD ENOUGH FOR HER?>

<I CAN'T UNDERSTAND WHY ANYONE WOULD THINK LIKE THAT, CAN YOU?>

<CAN YOU UNDERSTAND IT?>
<UH, NO, NOT AT ALL.>
<I SUPPOSE HE THOUGHT HE WAS PREVENTING HER FROM BEING TRULY HAPPY, PREVENTING HER FROM FINDING A "PERFECT SOMEONE.">
<BUT THERE IS NO "PERFECT SOMEONE.">
<NOTHING IN THE REAL WORLD EVER LIVES UP TO WHAT YOU FEEL INSIDE.>
<YOU JUST FIND HAPPINESS WHERE YOU CAN.>
<THANK YOU FOR HELPING US CLEAN UP, NANASAWA.>
<NO PROBLEM! I WAS GLAD TO HELP!>
<I'LL GO GET US SOME DRINKS. YOU TWO TAKE A BREAK.>
<OK.>
<THANK YOU!>
<WHEW, WHAT A DAY.>
<YEAH.>
PH34R MY L33T NINJA F33T OF FURY!!!
<WAS THAT-->
<I DIDN'T HEAR ANYTHING.>

<SO, YOU AND LARGO-SAN ARE STUCK HERE UNTIL YOU CAN EARN ENOUGH MONEY TO BUY TICKETS HOME?>
<YEAH.>
<THAT'S TERRIBLE. I DON'T KNOW IF I COULD DEAL WITH A PROBLEM LIKE THAT.>
<IT'S NOT THAT BAD. AT LEAST I HAVE A JOB AND A PLACE TO STAY.>
<I REALLY OWE HAYASAKA-SAN A LOT FOR HELPING US OUT AS MUCH AS SHE HAS.>
<I'M SURPRISED THAT SHE DIDN'T JUST GET TICKETS FOR YOU.>
<ERIKA DOES STUFF LIKE THAT.>
<ACTUALLY... I DON'T THINK I'D ACCEPT THEM.>
<IT'S MY FAULT WE'RE HERE, SO I'M THE ONE WHO SHOULD WORK HARD TO FIX IT.>
PREP4R3 FOR PANTLESS NINJ4 FURY!!!!
<THOUGH I MIGHT BE OK WITH HER PAYING TO HAVE LARGO SHIPPED HOME IN A CRATE.>
<STOP, THAT'D BE MEAN!>

"PANTLESS NINJA FURY?"
YES.
FR33 OF THE RESTRAINING CONFINES OF P4NTS, I WILL NOW TAKE YOU DOWN.
JUST WHAT EVERY GIRL LIKES TO HEAR.
HUAH! YOUR FACE! INTO T3H SAND!!
OK, YOU'VE BEATEN ME NINE TIMES OUT OF TEN ALL AFTERNOON.
WHAT'S WITH THE OUTBURSTS ALL OF A SUDDEN? RUBBING IT IN?
NO.
YOU'RE NOT JUST MASHING BUTTONS ANYMORE, YOU'RE PLAYING.
IT'S NO FUN PLAYING SOMEONE WHO ISN'T COMMITTED TO THE GAME.
<AH, THERE YOU ARE.>
<THERE'S FOOD AND BEER UP FRONT IF YOU'RE HUNGRY.>
FOOD AND BEER.
FOOD AND B33R?
<YOU KNOW, I DON'T ACTUALLY REMEMBER SEEING HIM DO ANYTHING TO HELP US TODAY.>
<YOU JUST DIDN'T SEE IT.>

<I SEE YOU WENT ALL OUT ON THE CHEAP 7-11 BENTOU.>
WOO! B33R IN A CAN!
<HEY, DON'T KNOCK IT. LOTTA PEOPLE LIVE OFFA' THIS STUFF.>
WHAT MANNER OF FOOD IS THIS?
IT'S BENTOU. A BOX LUNCH. JUST EAT IT.
<DOES LARGO-SAN LIKE JAPANESE FOOD?>
<ARE YOU FEELING ANY BETTER, ERIKA?>
<I'LL LIVE.>
<WE WERE ALL WORRIED ABOUT YOU.>
IT'S NOT GOING TO BITE YOU. JUST EAT IT.
<YES, WE WERE.
<WE ALL KNOW YOU CAN TAKE CARE OF YOURSELF, HAYASAKA.>
<BUT YOU SHOULD KNOW THAT WE'RE ALL HERE FOR YOU, AND WE'LL BACK YOU UP ANY TIME YOU NEED IT.>
HRM. AN UNUSUAL TASTE.

<THAT'S RIGHT!>
<SO, HERE'S TO YOU, YOU BIG PAIN IN THE BUTT.>
KAMPAI!
KAMPAI!!
WOOT! CH33RZ!!

YOU GONNA DRINK THAT?
MEGAGAMERS
YES.
YES I AM.

Conscience Enforcement Authority
Central Operations and Control
SPECIAL AGENT SERAPHIM?
OPERATIONS AGENT MARCUS. NICE TO SEE YOU.
HOW GOES THE BUSINESS OF DENYING EVERY BUDGET REQUEST MADE BY FIELD OPERATIVES?
FINE, FINE. I DIDN'T KNOW YOU WERE HERE.
JUST TAKING CARE OF A FEW THINGS.
I HEAR YOU HAD SOME UNWANTED ASSISTANCE RECENTLY.
YES, BUT THAT'S BEEN DEALT WITH.
I HAD A LITTLE TALK WITH THE DIRECTOR ABOUT OPERATIONAL SECURITY AND INTEGRITY
FUN. HOW GOES THE FIELD WORK?
GOOD. THERE IS MEASURABLE PROGRESS IN BOTH CASES.
EXCELLENT. SO DOES THAT MEAN YOU CAN RELAX A LITTLE? GO BACK TO FLYIN' SOLO? EASE OFF ON THE BUDGET REQUESTS?
HMMM? OH NO, NOT AT ALL.
BOTH OF THESE CASES ARE JUST STARTING TO GET INTERESTING.
SHALL WE GO, TEMPORARY SPECIAL AGENT BOO?
SQUEEK!
END - CHAPTER 5

Megatokyo
leave it to seraphim!

A FASHION TRIP 'ROUND THE WORLD!

I GET A LOT OF EMAILS TELLING ME THAT WE SPEND WAY TOO MUCH TIME TALKING ABOUT JAPAN.
I AGREE! LET'S FIND OUT WHAT AVERAGE PEOPLE WEAR IN OTHER PARTS OF THE WORLD!
LET'S TAKE A LITTLE "FASHION TRIP" SHALL WE?

OUR FIRST STOP, AUSTRALIA!
G'DAY MATE!
KOALA ACCESSORY OPTIONAL.

NEXT WE VISIT CHINA!
NI HAO!
CAREFUL! MANY CHINESE ACCES-SORIES CAN BE SHARP OR DANGER-OUS!
MERRY OLE ENGLAND!
GREETINGS, SUBJECTS.
ENGLISH ACCES-SORIES CAN BE HEAVY AND EXPENSIVE!

CANADA!
IT'S WARM BECAUSE IT'S STUFFED WITH FEATHERS, EH?
CANADIAN WINTER WEAR AND SUMMER WEAR ARE THE SAME THING.
ROOTS

RUSSIA!
THESE FURS AREN'T REAL ARE THEY?
THIS IS FAKE FUR, RIGHT?
SAME GOES FOR RUSSIA.

BRAZIL!!
AND FOR RIO TOO!
AMAZING WHAT YOU CAN LEARN ABOUT THE WORLD JUST FROM WATCHING MOVIES AND TV, ISN'T IT?
MAKES YOU WANNA ACTUALLY SEE IT.
SQUEEK.

メガトーキョー
megatokyo
chapter 6:
"operational insecurity"
Ninja Headquarters* - Tokyo
<ALL KNOW IT NINJA DUTY TO MONITOR ALL MORTAL COMBAT VISA HOLDER IN JAPAN.>
<HIGH AUTHORITY PASS DOWN DECISION THAT MORTAL COMBAT VISA HOLDER "LARGO" NOW RECOGNIZED AS THREAT TO BALANCE OF CHAOS IN JAPAN.>
<MISSION TO NEUTRALIZE THREAT IMPORTANT DUTY AND WELCOME CONTRACT IN TIME OF RECESSION.>
*actually, this not Ninja Headquarters. This just random building in Tokyo. We cannot show real Ninja Headquarters. Sorry.
<HEAD NINJA UNDERSTAND JUNPEI NOT WISH TO ACCEPT ASSIGNED MISSION.>
<HEAD NINJA REALIZE THIS MATTER OF PERSONAL HONOR, AND ACCEPT JUNPEI DECISION.>
<THANK YOU, HEAD NINJA.>
<HEAD NINJA SUPPORT JUNPEI IN JOURNEY TO LEARN "WAY OF L33T.">
<YET JUNPEI MUST UNDERSTAND THAT MISSION WILL BE ASSIGNED TO OTHER NINJA OR SUBCONTRACTOR>
<UNDERSTOOD, HEAD NINJA.>
<NO DISHONOR, BUT THIS "L33T MASTER" IS TOTAL NUTJOB.>
<JUNPEI SURE NOT ACCEPT MISSION?>
<PATH TO ENLIGHTENMENT CAN MAKE ENLIGHTENED ONES COMPLEX AND MISUNDERSTOOD, HEAD NINJA.>

<HERE YOU GO.>
<THANK YOU, HAYASAKA-SAMA! YOU HAVE NO IDEA HOW MUCH THIS MEANS TO ME!!>
<ANYTHING ELSE I CAN DO FOR YOU?>
<UHM, ER... I... UH...>
<NO, THAT'S OK! I'M ALL SET! THANK YOU SO MUCH, HAYASAKA-SAMA!!>
<BYE NOW!>
<STRANGE. THERE HAS BEEN A STEADY STREAM OF FANS ALL DAY, BUT THEY COME IN ONE AT A TIME.>
<YEAH, AND THEY ALL BUY SOME-THING.>
<TOO BAD WE DON'T HAVE ANY *GIRL PHASE* STUFF.>
<I FIGURED THAT I'D HAVE TO DEAL WITH A HUGE CROWD AGAIN TODAY.>
<SO FAR, THIS HASN'T BEEN SO BAD.>
<IS THAT WHY TODAY YOU WORE A COSPLAY OUTFIT THAT COMES WITH A BIG HELMET?>
<ACT-UALLY, THE HELMET IS FOR YOU.>
<ME?>
<NANASAWA SAID TO MAKE SURE YOU WEAR IT. SHE SEEMS TO THINK YOU ARE PRONE TO HEAD INJURIES.>
HFC
CUTELAB

<HM.>
<I FIGURED LARGO WOULD BE OUT HERE BEATING PEOPLE UP, BUT HE'S NOT.>
<HEH.>

<DID MASAMICHI HIRE YOU OR WAS THIS LARGO'S IDEA?>
<NINJA OFTEN HIRED FOR CROWD CONTROL. JUNPEI SENT TO MANAGE CROWD AS MATTER OF PUBLIC SAFETY.>
<SO, MASAMICHI HIRED YOU.>
<JUNPEI NOT ALLOWED SAY.>

<IS LARGO UPSTAIRS?>
<I THINK SO. THE DOOR IS STILL BLOCKED, SO THE ONLY WAY OUT IS THROUGH THE STORE.>
<I HAVEN'T SEEN HIM SNEAK OUT YET.>
<WHAT WAS HE DOING LAST NIGHT?>
<LAST NIGHT? WELL, UH...>
<ACTUALLY...>
<HE WANTED TO KNOW MORE ABOUT YOU.>
<HE WHAT?>
<HE WANTED ME TO TELL HIM ALL I KNOW ABOUT YOU AND YOUR CAREER.>
<I WAS KINDA SURPRISED, LARGO USUALLY ISN'T INTO STUFF LIKE THIS.>
<WE WENT ONLINE AND AND I SHOWED HIM ALL OF THE ANIME THAT YOU'VE HAD VOICE PARTS IN, THE CDS YOU MADE, YOUR CONCERTS, EVENTS, AND EVEN YOUR RADIO SHOW.>
<HE HAD ALREADY FOUND ALL KINDS OF FAN SITES AND BULLETIN BOARDS, BUT WE WENT LOOKING FOR MORE.>
<IT'S PRETTY AMAZING WHAT YOU CAN FIND ONLINE IF YOU KNOW WHERE TO LOOK.>
<SO, YOU ACTUALLY HELPED HIM.>
<UH HUH! LARGO SEEMED PARTICULARLY INTERESTED IN THE FAN SITES FOR SOME REASON.>
<ONCE I SHOWED HIM A WEBSITE THAT WOULD TRANSLATE EVERYTHING INTO ENGLISH, HE WAS ABLE TO...>
<UH...>
<PUT THE HELMET ON, PIRO.>
<Y...Y... YES MA'AM.>

LARGO, I'D LIKE A WORD WITH YOU.
LARGO?
AH.
IT'S YOU.
I HAVE A NAME, YOU KNOW.
I SEE YOU ARE UN-DAMAGED.
WHY ARE YOU HELPING YOUR LITTLE FRIEND TRACK DOWN AND BULLY FANBOYS?
JUNPEI ASKED ME TO HELP HIM.
I THOUGHT I TOLD YOU--
JUNPEI HAD BEEN ORDERED TO KEEP EVERYONE AWAY FROM YOU AND THE STORE.
I INSISTED THAT YOU HAD THE RIGHT TO FIGHT YOUR OWN BATTLES.
JUNPEI AGREED. TOGETHER WE HAVE WORKED ONLY TO KEEP YOU FROM BEING OVERWHELMED BY AN UNCHECKED HORDE.
TAK TAK TAK
I TOLD YOU THAT I DO NOT WANT YOU OR ANYONE ELSE PROTECTING ME!
WHAT PART OF THAT DON'T YOU UNDER-STAND?
I AM NOT TRYING TO PROTECT YOU, I AM TRYING TO OPEN YOUR EYES!!
OPEN MY EYES TO WHAT?
YOUR WEAKNESSES.

OH BOY. I THINK HAYASAKA-SAN IS MAD AT ME.
I DIDN'T WANT HER TO KNOW THAT I USED TO BE A BIG FAN, BUT I THINK SHE KNOWS NOW.
WHY DID I TELL HER ABOUT WHAT I TOLD LARGO LAST NIGHT?
WHY DID I DO THAT?
CUTELAB
(SIGH)
I AM SO STUPID.
MAYBE SHE'S UPSET BECAUSE SHE WANTED LARGO TO GET TO KNOW HER FOR WHO SHE IS, NOT WHAT SHE USED TO BE.
HUH? WHAT DO YOU MEAN?
DON'T YOU THINK SHE SEEMED TOUCHED, JUST FOR A MOMENT, WHEN YOU TOLD HER THAT LARGO HAD ASKED ABOUT HER?
I WONDER...
THEY SPENT A LOT OF TIME TOGETHER YESTERDAY, PLAYING GAMES AND HANGING OUT IN THE BACK ROOM.
LARGO HAS BEEN ACTING VERY PROTECTIVE OF HER, IN HIS OWN, IDIOTIC SORT OF WAY.
ERIKA DID SPECIFICALLY ASK YOU ABOUT LARGO THIS MORNING...
PLEASE... PLEASE STOP.
OH, FOO. YOU THINK YOU ARE THE ONLY ONE ALLOWED TO SHOW INTEREST IN GIRLS?
GET OVER YOURSELF.
CUTELAB

SEE?
THOUSANDS UPON THOUSANDS OF MINDLESS ZOMBIES OBSESSING OVER YOUR EVERY MOVE. THEY ARE NETWORKED. THEY ARE ORGANIZED. THEY ARE OBSESSED.
HERE IS A PICTURE OF YOU AT THE 7-11 DOWN THE STREET TAKEN AT 9AM THIS MORNING.
HERE IS A PHOTO GALLERY THAT INDEXES THE KIND OF SOCKS YOU WEAR, ORGANIZED BY DATE.
THAT IS WHAT FANS DO, LARGO. THERE'S NOTHING I CAN DO ABOUT IT.
IT IS DANGEROUS FOR A HORDE OF THIS SIZE TO HAVE READY ACCESS TO ALL THIS DATA.
YOU DO NOT GRASP THE EXTENT OF YOUR VULNERABLITIES IN THE DIGITAL PLANE.
IF JUNPEI HAD NOT BEEN ABLE TO ACT UPON THE DATA I GATHERED THIS MORNING, YOU WOULD HAVE BEEN OVERWHELMED BY THE HORDE THAT DESCENDED ON YOU.
I WOULD HAVE DEALT WITH IT.
THE SAME WAY YOU DEALT WITH YESTERDAY'S HORDE?
ALL RIGHT, SO HOW **DO** I DEAL WITH THIS?
YOU'RE THE COMPUTER EXPERT, YOU TELL ME.
I HAVE THE RESOURCES, I WILL MAKE SURE THAT--
NO.
I WILL DO IT MY-SELF.
SHOW ME.

SHOW...
YOU?
YOU HEARD ME. SHOW ME HOW TO DO IT.
I CANNOT GIVE YOU ACCESS TO TOOLS YOU DO NOT FULLY UNDERSTAND HOW TO USE! MUCH 3VIL IS DONE BY THE WAYWARD ACTIONS OF THE UNSKILLED!
FINE, THEN I'LL LEARN HOW TO USE THEM.
IT TAKES YEARS TO MASTER TH3 M4D L33T SKILLZ J00 WILL N33D.
IT WILL TAKE LONGER IF YOU KEEP RANTING AT ME LIKE A MORON.
WHAT SYSTEMS DO YOU POSSESS?
SYSTEMS? I DON'T ACTUALLY HAVE A COMPUTER RIGHT NOW.
I'LL GO TO AKIHABARA THIS AFTERNOON AND BUY ONE.
YOU WOULD ACTUALLY PURCHASE...
A PRE-ASSEMBLED SYSTEM??
WOULD YOU RATHER I STEAL IT?
PRE-ASSEMBLED BOXES ARE AN ABOMINATION! THEY ARE AN AFFRONT TO ALL THAT IS L33T!!
A BOX MUST BE HAND CRAFTED TO FIT THE NEEDS OF THE INDIVIDUAL! PARTS MUST BE CAREFULLY SELECTED, LOVINGLY ASSEMBLED, AND TUNED WITH THE UTMOST SKILL!
ONLY THEN WILL YOUR BOX BE A DEVICE WORTHY OF BEING AN EXTENSION OF YOUR PHYSICAL SELF!
I WILL BUILD YOU A MACHINE.
NO, NO YOU WILL NOT.

TADAIMA, PIRO-KUN!
IT CAN'T BE. NO WAY.
THERE'S NO WAY...

<OH, HEY PING. HOW WAS YOUR SLEEP-OVER?>
<IT WAS FUN! WE STAYED UP AND TALKED AND PLAYED GAMES ALL NIGHT!>
<THAT'S GOOD.>

<I WAS SO HAPPY WHEN YOU CALLED TO CHECK UP ON ME.>
<THAT WAS SO SWEET!>

<UHH... ER, YEAH.>
<SO, HOW IS... TOHYA-SAN? IS THAT HER NAME?>
<SHE'S DOING GOOD! SHE SAID TO SAY HI TO YOU AND LARGO-SAN.>

<OH, AND SHE WANTED ME TO GIVE YOU SOME-THING.>

<HERE YA GO!>
cave of evil
PASS

"CAVE OF EVIL - <ONE FREE PASS.>"

CAVE OF EVIL.
<UH HUH! THERE'S ONE FOR BOTH OF US!>
<TOHYA-SAN WORKS THERE AND SAYS IT'S REALLY FUN!>

<SO... WHY IS SHE GIVING ME ONE?>
<WELL, TOHYA-SAN WANTS US TO COME SEE HER TONIGHT, SO... THEY'RE FOR US!>
<THIS SAYS IT'S IN HARAJUKU. WHAT IS IT? SOME SORT OF CLUB?>
<CAN WE GO, PIRO-KUN? PLEASE? TOHYA-SAN REALLY WANTS US TO.>
<PLEASE?>
<PLEASE?>
<OK, OK, SURE. IT'S NOT LIKE I HAVE ANY OTHER PLANS.>
<HEY.>
<YOU OK, NANA-SAWA?>
<SOMETIMES IT'S HARD TO TELL IF YOU'RE ACTING OR ACTUALLY UPSET SOMETIMES.>
<I'M SORRY! IS... IS IT TOO MUCH?>
<NO, NOT AT ALL. YOU ARE VERY... REAL ABOUT IT, WHICH MAKES IT THAT MUCH MORE INTENSE SOMEHOW.>
<YOU'RE EVEN GETTIN' TO AN OLD CYNIC LIKE ME.>
<YOU'RE KINDA SCARY, NANA-SAWA.>
<I'M SORRY.>
<DON'T BE. YOU'RE DOING GREAT.>
<UHN.>
<UHM, I HATE TO SPRING THIS ON YOU SO SUDDENLY, BUT I HAD A CHANCE TO GET YOU ON AOI MUMU'S RADIO SHOW TONIGHT, SO I DID.>
<NINE O'CLOCK.>
<REEEHHHHHH????>
<EXCEL-LENT! A CUTE, FRENETIC PANIC!>
<THAT'S EXACTLY WHAT THE NEXT SCENE CALLS FOR!>

NO! I WILL NOT TOLERATE YOU USING L4M3 EQUIPMENT!!
ALL RIGHT, ALL RIGHT! FINE!
JUST... SHOW ME WHAT TO DO AND I'LL BUILD IT MYSELF.
BUILD IT YOURSELF?
ARE YOU GONNA TELL ME THAT I CAN'T?
HEH.
MOST BOXES ARE ASSEMBLED FROM STANDARD COMPONENTS.
ONLY BY BUILDING IT YOURSELF CAN YOU BE SURE THAT EVERY COMPONENT IS L33T. W34K COMPONENTS WILL CRIPPLE YOUR MACHINE.
ALSO, IT IS NOT ENOUGH TO JUST BUY L33T COMPONENTS. YOU MUST SELECT THEM WITH SKILL AND ASSEMBLE THEM WITH CARE.
I WILL NOW SHOW YOU WHAT THESE COMPONENTS ARE AND DEMONSTRATE HOW THEY GO TOGETHER.
TAKE OFF YOUR CLOTHES.
WHAT?
STATIC CAN BE DEADLY TO SENSITIVE COMPONENTS.
THE AMOUNT OF STATIC GENERATED BY THAT MUCH FABRIC COULD POWER A SMALL VILLAGE.
OFF WITH IT.

<WHERE IS HAYASAKA-SAN? THAT'S THE FIFTH FAN TO COME IN SINCE SHE LEFT.>
<I THINK SHE'S STILL UPSTAIRS.>
<SHE IS?>
<UH HUH! I WAS SWEEPING IN THE COSPLAY SECTION WHEN HAYASAKA-SAN CAME DOWN THE LADDER AND ASKED ME TO HELP HER FIND SOMETHING MORE COMFORTABLE TO WEAR.>
<MORE COMFORT-ABLE??
<UH HUH. AFTER SHE CHANGED, SHE WENT BACK UP THE LADDER.>
<SHE... CHANGED???>
<UH HUH!>
<THEY WERE JUST THE CUTEST LITTLE GYM SHORTS!>
-THONK-
<HAYASAKA-SAN HAS SUCH A NICE FIGURE. I'M SO JEALOUS!>
<OH! HI, HAYASAKA-SAN!>
<HI PING.>
<PIRO, DID YOU SEE WHAT I DID WITH MY BACK PACK?>
<IM PRETTY SURE IT'S NOT ON MY BACK SO YOU CAN STOP LOOKING THERE.>
<TRY LOOKING UNDER THE COUNTER.>

<IT WAS IN THE BACK ROOM.>
<AH. THANK YOU.>
<SOME-THING WRONG?>
<NO, NOTHING, NOTHING.>
<I HAVE TO GO OUT FOR A BIT.>
<WATCH THE STORE.>
OK.
<PIRO-KUN, WHAT'S WRONG?>
<YOU LOOK UNHAPPY.>
<I DUNNO, IT'S JUST...>
<LARGO AND ERIKA? I JUST DON'T SEE IT.>
<HOW CAN SHE STAND HIM? I MEAN, HE DOESN'T EVEN ACKNOW-LEDGE THAT WOMEN EXIST, NEVER MIND... NEVER MIND...>
<NO, I CAN'T GO THERE. I DON'T WANT TO THINK ABOUT IT.>
<GEEP!>
SO, SHE WAS SERIOUS AFTER ALL.
<KYAAAAAA!!!>
<GYAH!>

HM. SHE IS TALKING TO MY NINJ4.
LARGO! GET... GET AWAY FROM THE DOOR!
WHAT ARE YOU DOING?
I NEED TO KNOW WHICH WAY SHE IS GOING SO I CAN FOLLOW HER.
FOLLOW HER??
LARGO, WHAT'S GOING ON?
CUTE LAB
SHE NEEDS A COMPUTER, AND ASKED MY ADVICE ON WHAT TO GET.
SHE WAS IMPRESSED WITH MY L33T EQUIPMENT, SO SHE ASKED ME TO SHOW HER HOW TO BUILD ONE.
WAIT...
YOU DIDN'T ASK HER TO...
GET NAKED...
DID YOU?
SHE REFUSED TO GET COMPLETELY N4KED, BUT I WAS STILL ABLE TO SHOW HER WHAT TO DO WITHOUT DAMAGING MY GEAR.
NOW SHE IS ON A QUEST TO PURCHASE COMPONENTS FOR HER OWN BOX.
I TOLD HER THAT SHE LACKS THE SKILLZ NECESSARY TO BUY PARTS WITHOUT HELP, BUT SHE REFUSED TO LET ME ACCOMPANY HER.
I CAN'T THINK OF **ANY** REASON WHY SHE WOULDN'T WANT TO BE SEEN IN PUBLIC WITH YOU.
<PIRO-KUN, IT'S BEEN 270 SECONDS.>
<I HAVE TO START HITTING HIM NOW.>

<HOLD ON, PING, WAIT.>
SO, NOTHING HAPPENED UP THERE? NOTHING AT ALL?
THERE WAS NO STATIC DISCHARGE, SO NONE OF MY CHIPSETS WERE DAMAGED.
THAT'S NOT WHAT I MEANT.
YOU DIDN'T DO ANYTHING CATACLYSMICALLY STUPID, DID YOU?
I DON'T THINK SO.
THERE WILL BE SOME DIFFERENCES BETWEEN THE XEON P2/550 BOX I DEMONSTRATED ASSEMBLY TECHNIQUE ON AND THE PARTS SHE WILL BE ACQUIRING.
BUT I THINK SHE WILL BE ABLE TO APPLY WHAT I SHOWED HER.
OK. SO, IT WAS JUST A COMPUTER BUILDING. LESSON.
RIGHT.
OK.
SHE'S REALLY SOFT.
I MEAN, LIKE... **WOW** KINDA SOFT.
ESPECIALLY HER LEGS.
OH, AND HER BOOBS ARE **REALLY** SOFT!
<PIRO-KUN, I HAVE TO KEEP MY EYES CLOSED WHILE I TRY TO HIT HIM. YOU SHOULD MOVE.>

YOU PSYCHOTIC SONY!!!
WACK!
ECCHI!!
WACK!
AWAY FROM ME--
WACK!
SUKEBE!!
WACK!
GET--
HENTAI!!!
<AH... PIRO-KUN?>
<THE BROOM. IT KINDA... BROKE. HEH.>
<WHAT-EVER.>
<I'M SORRY! DON'T BE MAD! I DIDN'T MEAN TO BREAK IT!>
<FORGET THE STUPID BROOM, PING.>
KEEP THAT INSANE MACHINE FROM ATTACKING ME.
I'M GOING FOR THE DOOR.
IT MAY BE TOO LATE FOR ME TO FIND HER AND FOLLOW HER.
DAMN THAT PLASTIC TOY OF YOURS.
UH, LARGO...
GOOD LUCK.
THERE IS NO SUCH THING AS LUCK, ONLY SKILLZ.
I'LL BE BACK.

TRIXBOX
<THAT'S SOME PRETTY SERIOUS HARDWARE MA'AM.>
<AND YOU SAY THAT YOU'VE NEVER BUILT YOUR OWN SYSTEM BEFORE?>
TRIXBOX
<NO. IS THERE ANYTHING ELSE I'LL NEED?>
<YOU KNOW, WE HAVE A LOT OF FINE PRE-BUILT SYSTEMS THAT CAN SAVE YOU THE HASSLE AND DIFFICULTY OF TRYING TO BUILD ONE FROM SCRATCH.>
<FOR EXAMPLE, HOW ABOUT THIS BRAND NEW APPLE MAC MINI?>
<IT'S SIMPLE, EASY TO USE, AND GREAT FOR EMAIL AND WEB BROWSING!>
<JUST LOOK AT THIS CUTE LITTLE BOX!>
<IT REALLY SUITS A PRETTY GIRL LIKE YOU.>
<I'LL EVEN GIVE YOU A SPECIAL DISCOUNT.>
<DO I STILL GET THE DISCOUNT IF I USE IT TO BREAK YOUR JAW?>

SO, ARE YOU DEPRESSED BECAUSE YOUR FRIEND IS HOT FOR A GIRL YOU LIKE?
NO, NO, IT'S COOL.
ARE YOU UPSET BECAUSE YOU THINK YOUR FRIEND IS MAKING MORE PROGRESS WITH THIS GIRL THAN YOU THINK YOU ARE WITH KIMIKO?
WELL?
ARE YOU MAD BECAUSE YOU CAN'T GO ON AND BRAG ABOUT HOW SOFT SOME OF KIMIKO'S PARTS MIGHT BE?
NO, I AM NOT.
<PIRO-KUN?>
<THERE'S A CELL PHONE RINGING IN THE BAG THAT I PUT HAYASAKA-SAN'S CLOTHES IN. SHOULD I ANSWER IT?>
<YEAH, SURE.>
THIS ISN'T A RACE, PIRO. GOOD RELATIONSHIPS TAKE TIME TO BUILD.
bingbingbibibing
IF YOU WANT TO WIN A GIRL'S HEART, YOU NEED TO TREAT HER LIKE A REAL PERSON, NOT SOME OBJECT YOU WANT TO PUT ON A PEDESTAL.
きみこ
<OOPS, I GUESS I MISSED ANSWERING IT, PIRO-KUN.>
-SNAPCLICK-

IT IS AS I PH34R3D.
THEY WILL NOT ALLOW HER TO PURCHASE L33T COMPONENTS WITHOUT BEING ABLE TO EXPRESS OBSESSION WITH THEM.
I WILL HAVE TO HEAD HER OFF AT THE NEXT STORE.
<HOLY... THAT MUST BE HER.>
<WOW. YEAH, SHE IS HOT.>
<SO, D'YA THINK THAT GUY WAS SERIOUS? DO YOU THINK HE'D REALLY... IF WE DON'T-->
<YES MA'AM! WHAT CAN I DO FOR YOU?>
<UH... WOW. MA'AM, THESE ARE EXPENSIVE COMPONENTS.>
<ARE YOU SURE THAT-->
<OK! I EVEN THINK WE HAVE EVERYTHING IN STOCK!>
<I'LL GO GET THE MEMORY!>
<OK! IS THERE ANYTHING ELSE WE CAN DO FOR YOU MA'AM? ANY QUESTIONS?>
<DO I HAVE TO BE COMPLETELY NAKED TO HANDLE THESE PARTS SAFELY? IF I STRIP DOWN TO MY UNDERWEAR, IS THAT ENOUGH?>
<NO! NO! YOU MUST BE NAKED!!!>
<THAT DEPENDS!! PLEASE DESCRIBE THE UNDER-GARMENTS!!>

<SOMEONE MUST REALLY NEED TO TALK TO HAYASAKA-SAN. IT'S RINGING AGAIN.>
<MAYBE I SHOULD ANSWER IT.>

<IT'S... NANASAWA SAN!>

<HELLO?>
<ERIKA!?!>

<NANASAWA-SAN? THIS IS PIRO.>
<PIRO-SAN?? IS ERIKA THERE? I NEED TO TO TALK TO HER!>
<SHE WENT OUT ABOUT AN HOUR AGO. I DON'T KNOW WHEN SHE'LL BE BACK.>
<SHE LEFT HER CELL PHONE HERE.>
<SHE DID?>

<UWAHEEE... WHAT AM I GONNA DO??>
<WHAT'S WRONG? WHAT HAPPENED?>
<I'M GONNA BE ON THE RADIO!!>
<THE WHAT? THE RADIO?>

<I'M GONNA BE ON AOI MUMU'S RADIO SHOW TONIGHT, AND I WANTED TO ASK ERIKA FOR SOME ADVICE.>
<MUMU-CHAN'S SHOW? REALLY?? THAT'S AWESOME!>
<YEAH, BUT I'VE NEVER DONE ANYTHING LIKE THIS BEFORE! I DON'T KNOW WHAT I SHOULD DO, OR SAY, OR...>
<UWAHEE... I'M SO NERVOUS.>
<DON'T BE, NANASAWA-SAN, YOU'LL BE FINE!>

<I MEAN, I DON'T KNOW ANYTHING ABOUT RADIO SHOWS, BUT...>
<THEY ARE USUALLY BEST WHEN PEOPLE HAVE FUN AND JUST BE THEM-SELVES.>
<JUST BE YOURSELF, SAY WHAT YOU FEEL, AND YOU'LL BE FINE!>

<BE MYSELF? BUT... I'M NOT A VERY INTERESTING PERSON! I DON'T HAVE ANY KIND OF PERSONALITY!>
<HOW CAN YOU SAY THAT? YOU'VE GOT TONS OF PERSONALITY! A HELL OF A LOT MORE THAN I DO, THAT'S FOR SURE!>
<SHE'LL WANT TO TALK ABOUT STUPID, INANE THINGS AND I'LL HAVE TO TRY TO SOUND CUTE AND I'M NOT GOOD AT THAT.>
<SURE YOU ARE! I'D LISTEN TO YOU TALK ABOUT STUPID THINGS ALL DAY LONG!>
<BUT...>
<NANASAWA, STUDIO TIME IS EXPENSIVE. LET'S GO.>
<OK!>
<I HAVE TO GO! BYE!>
<AEHH...>
OH GOD.
PLEASE TELL ME THAT CONVERSATION DIDN'T HAPPEN. PLEASE TELL ME I DIDN'T SAY ALL THOSE STUPID THINGS TO HER.
SHE HAS GOT TO THINK I'M A RAVING IDIOT NOW...
<PIRO-KUN?>
<I CAN'T UNDER-STAND WHAT YOU ARE SAY-ING....>
I... I DON'T THINK WELL ENOUGH ON MY FEET TO TALK TO HER ON THE PHONE! THIS IS A BIG NIGHT FOR HER! I DON'T WANT TO RUIN IT!
<PING! DO NOT LET ME ANSWER THIS PHONE IF IT RINGS AGAIN!>
<WE HAVE TO FIND-->
bingbingbibibing...bing...bibibing....bingbingbibibi

AREN'T YOU AFRAID?

AREN'T YOU AFRAID SOME-ONE MIGHT RECOGNIZE YOU AND SHOUT OUT WHO YOU ARE?
AKIHABARA IS A CENTER OF OTAKU DEPRAVITY. IF I WERE A IDOL IN HIDING, I'D BE TERRIFIED TO COME HERE.

AREN'T YOU AFRAID I MIGHT BASH IN YOUR SKULL WITH ONE OF THESE BAGS?
AH, YOUR INFAMOUS VIOLENT TENDENCIES.
THEY ARE THE STUFF OF LEGEND IN THE INDUSTRY. IF ONLY YOUR FANS KNEW.

YOU REALIZE THAT YOUR POPULARITY HAS NOT YET RUN ITS COURSE.
IF YOU WISH IT TO END, YOU HAVE TO EMBRACE IT AND SEE IT THROUGH.

UNLIKE YOUR FORMER HANDLERS, WE AT SEGA COULD PROVIDE YOU WITH SUPERIOR PROTECTION AGAINST--
WHAT THE?
RRRRRRRRRRRRRRRRRA

OW.
KWUMP!
MISTER MUFFIN
VRRRRRR

A TRUCK WOULD HAVE BEEN MORE SATISFYING.

OOF.

VRMMM...
RWIP!
CLICK

IT'S BEEN A LONG TIME SINCE YOU'VE RUN ME DOWN WITH A MOTORIZED VEHICLE. BRINGS BACK MEMORIES.

YOU STARTED THAT RIOT YESTERDAY.

WHY? WHAT'S YOUR GAME?

LARGO, LARGO, LARGO. A MINION ALREADY?

DON'T YOU SEE THE AWESOME POWER SHE POSSESSES? SHE'S EVEN CAPABLE OF SUBJUGATING AND CONTROLLING SOMEONE LIKE YOU.

AMAZING. *SEGA* MUST HAVE HER.

YOU WILL STAY AWAY FROM HER OR NEXT TIME I'LL USE A LAWNMOWER.

OHHH, LOOK AT YOU, OUT RUNNING PEOPLE DOWN TO PROTECT YOUR NEW GIRLYFRIEND.

WUSS.

SHE'S NOT A PERSON, LARGO, SHE'S A COMMODITY.
BE HAPPY FOR HER. AT LEAST COMMODITIES ARE WORTH SOME-THING.

OH, AND BY THE WAY - WERE YOU AWARE THAT THE *TPCD* PUT A CONTRACT OUT ON YOU? NINJA CORPORATION HAD THE LOWEST BID AND WON THE CONTRACT.

IT'S AMAZING HOW LITTLE THEY'LL WORK FOR.
ALMOST INSULTING, REALLY.
GOOD LUCK!
SEGA

<PIRO-KUN!>
bingbingbibibing...bing...bibibing....bingbingbibibing...bing...bibibing....
bingbingbibibing...bing...
<NANASAWA, CAN'T THAT WAIT?>
<UHM, PIRO...>
<WHAT THE HELL ARE YOU DOING?>
<IT... IT WENT TO VOICE MAIL.>
ngbingbibibing...
<I'M NOT ANSWERING MY PHONE RIGHT NOW.>
<LEAVE A MESSAGE.>
<PIRO-SAN? THANK YOU FOR TALKING TO ME, IT REALLY HELPED.>
<I'LL TRY TO RELAX AND NOT BE SO NERVOUS. I'LL BE MYSELF. I'LL PRETEND THAT IT'S JUST LIKE TALKING TO YOU, LIKE YOU'RE THE ONLY ONE LISTENING.>
<ERIKA, IF YOU GET THIS, CAN YOU GIVE THE PHONE TO PIRO-SAN?>
<IS IT OK IF I CALL YOU AGAIN? BEFORE I GO ON?>
<BOSS-SAN, IS HAYASAKA-SAN BACK YET>
<YOU'RE JOKING, RIGHT?>
<CAN YOU WATCH THE STORE? I HAVE TO TRY TO FIND HER!>
<IT'S AN EMERGENCY!>
<PLEASE BE THERE, OK?>
<I'LL BE BACK AS SOON AS I CAN!>
<PIRO-KUN?>

<I'LL NEVER FIND HER! I HAVE NO IDEA WHERE SHE WENT!>
MEGAGAMERS

<FRIEND OF L33T MASTER LOOK FOR SOMEONE?>
<Y...YES! A WOMAN WHO LEFT THE STORE OVER AN HOUR AGO!>
<BIG LONG PONY TAIL, JEANS, GREEN JACKET. DID YOU SEE WHICH WAY SHE WENT?>

<HAYASAKA-DONO.>
<SHE ASK JUNPEI NOT FOLLOW. SAY ASSISTANCE NOT NEEDED WHERE GOING.>
<L33T MASTER KNOW WHERE HAYASAKA-DONO GO. HE FOLLOW, TELL JUNPEI STAY, GUARD STORE.>

<DID LARGO TELL YOU WHERE SHE WENT? NANASAWA-SAN IS GONNA BE ON A RADIO SHOW TONIGHT AND REALLY NEEDS TO TALK TO HER!>
<IT'S REALLY IMPORTANT! THIS COULD REALLY AFFECT HER CAREER!>

<IF THERE'S ANYWAY YOU CAN HELP ME... PLEASE?>

<JUNPEI HELP FRIEND OF L33T MASTER.>
<GIRL COME WITH YOU? EDS UNIT HEAVY. JUNPEI NOT SURE ABLE CARRY BOTH TO AKIHABARA.>
<MANY ROOF IN OCHANOMIZU HAVE LOW LOAD LIMIT.>

<UM, SORRY...>
<DID YOU SAY... CARRY?>

<SAAA...>
<JUNPEI SORRY. WE TAKE SUBWAY.>
AGAMER

<ALL THAT'S LEFT IS A CASE, THE WATER COOLING SYSTEM, AND A FLAT SCREEN MONITOR.>
COMPUDOG
<HEY, ISN'T THAT...>
<OH MY GOD, I THINK IT IS!>
<HOW AM I GOING TO GET ALL OF THIS HOME?>
<AIEEE!!>
<GUWAHH!>
THUMP
MISTER MUFFIN
THUMP
<LOOK! IS THAT HAYASAKA-HIME?>
<WHERE, WHERE??>
<MAYBE...>
<RUN AWAY! RUN AWAY!!>

<WHERE'S MY CELLPHONE?>
<HERE, I'LL SEND YOU A PIC!>
<YOU'RE RIGHT! I THINK IT'S HER!>
<FEH.>
<HE'S PROBABLY BUSY ANYWAY.>
<KYAAAA!!!!!>
THUMP
THUMP
<OOOF!!>
THUMP
MISTER MUFFIN

<UHM... HAYASAKA-SAN?
<COULD MY FRIEND AND I GET YOUR AUTO-GRAPH?>
<IF IT'S NOT TOO MUCH TROUBLE, MA'AM.>
<UHM, SURE.>
<REAL QUICK, OK? I HAVE A LOT TO DO THIS AFTER-NOON.>
beep! beep!
VRRRM!
beep! beep!
VRRM!
VRRR
RRM VRRM! VRMVRM VRRRR
GYAH!!
HEY!!
RRRRRRRRRM!
IF THAT'S WHO I THINK IT IS, I'LL TIE THOSE BUNNY EARS AROUND HIS--
<ERIKA-CHAN?>
<M...MEIMI-SAN?>
<GOODNESS, IT'S BEEN A LONG TIME. HOW HAVE YOU BEEN, DEAR?>

FSK! WHAT IS SHE DOING!?
MISTER MUFFIN
WHY WILL SHE TAKE NO ACTION TO PROTECT HER-SELF?
L33T MASTER.
HAPPY
JUNPEI!
WHAT ARE JOO DOIN' HERE?
FRIEND OF L33T MASTER NEED FIND HAYASAKA-DONO.
SAY VERY IMPORTANT.
L33T MASTER KNOW WHERE FIND HAYASAKA-DONO?
HAPPY
JO DUDE, WHAT'S UP?
YEAH, SHE'S BACK THERE TALKING TO SOME LADY.
YOU'RE WEARING A "HAPPY VEGGIE" BUNNY SUIT.
PLEASE TELL ME WHY.
HAPPY
MY LIFE IS IN DANGER. I CANNOT RISK BEING SEEN.
THAT'S WHY I HAVE TO WEAR A DISGUISE. I DON'T HAVE L33T HIDING SKILLZ LIKE JUNPEI.
I CAN'T HIDE IN PLAIN SIGHT THE WAY NINJ4 CAN.

<THAT SOUNDS VERY NICE, BUT ARE YOU SURE YOU'RE DOING OK?>
<MASAMICHI AND I ARE WORRIED ABOUT YOU.>
<DON'T BE. I'M FINE.>
<SO... UHM... WHAT BRINGS YOU OUT THIS WAY?>
YOUR LIFE IS IN DANGER?
WHY? BECAUSE YOU BEAT UP SOME DELIVERY GUY AND STOLE HIS SCOOTER?
WHAT ABOUT THE RABBIT SUIT? DID YOU--
NO. I DON'T HAVE TIME FOR THIS. I HAVE TO TALK TO HAYASAKA-SAN!
PIRO, STOP! IT'S TOO DANGEROUS!!
<I'M JUST DOING SOME SHOPPING.>
<LOOK AT THIS BEAUTIFUL SET OF KITCHEN KNIVES I FOUND.>
<A REAL BARGAIN, TOO!>
<SHOPPING. I SHOULD HAVE GUESSED.>
<THOSE ARE NICE. HOW MUCH WERE THEY?>
WITLESS FOO!!
I HAVE TO STOP HIM BEFORE--
L33T MASTER, WAIT.
JUNPEI ADVISE EXTREME CAUTION.
SITUATION VERY DANGER-OUS.
<OH DEAR.>
<I BELIEVE I FORGOT TO PAY FOR THEM.>
<ARE YOU **STILL** DOING THAT?>
<HAYA-SAKA-SAN!!>

<PIRO? WHAT'S WRONG?>
<NANASAWA-SAN HAS BEEN TRYING TO GET A HOLD OF YOU BUT YOU LEFT YOUR CELL PHONE AT THE STORE!>
<SHE HAS? OK, I'LL CALL HER IN A FEW MINUTES.>
<HELLO, MY NAME IS SONODA MEIMI. NICE TO MEET YOU!>
<UHM, MEIMI-SAN, THIS IS PIRO.>
<HE WORKS AT *MEGA-GAMERS* WITH ME.>
<GOOD AFTER-NOON, NICE TO MEET YOU.>
<SO YOU MUST BE THE YOUNG AMERICAN ERIKA IS DATING. PLEASE TAKE GOOD CARE OF HER!>
<I'M SORRY... WHAT?>
<N-N-NO! THAT'D BE MY FRIEND LARGO, NOT ME!!>
ARE THEY REALLY THAT DANGEROUS?
YES L33T MASTER. AS DANGEROUS AS MOST SKILLED NINJA.
HAPPY
SUCH 3VIL...
SO, THESE "MAGICAL GRRLS," ARE THEY A FORCE OF ULTIMATE 3VIL?
NO, L33T MASTER, NOT 3VIL.
NINJA LIVE BY CODE OF HONOR.
MAGICAL GIRL LIVE BY CODE OF LOVE.
THIS LEAD TO MANY DISASTER AND MUCH DESTRUCTION OF URBAN AREA.
HONOR MUCH SAFER.
3VIL, HONOR OR LOV3, I WILL NOT LET IT MOCK ME.

WHAT?
EH?! UH, ER...
<PARDON ME! I AM SO SORRY! MASAMICHI DID SAY HE HAD RED HAIR. SO, IS THIS LARGO-SAN THEN?>
GAH! L-LARGO!
<MY MY, SUCH A SERIOUS YOUNG MAN.>
<PLEASE TAKE GOOD CARE OF OUR ERIKA, LARGO-SAN!>
<SHE WAS HURT VERY BADLY NOT LONG AGO. IT WAS LIKE SHE HAD LOST THE DESIRE TO LIVE HER LIFE.>
<MEIMI-SAN!>
<ERIKA, YOU HAVE NO IDEA HOW MUCH IT MEANS TO ME TO SEE YOU HAPPY AND FULL OF LIFE AGAIN!>
GIVE ME THE BAGS.
PROTECT YOURSELF.
<I'M SORRY, DID I SAY SOMETHING WRONG?>
<IS THIS A BAD TIME?>
<N...NO! NOT AT ALL! WE WERE JUST OUT SHOPPING...>
<AND STUFF.>
<LARGO-SAN DOESN'T SPEAK ANY JAPANESE, SO PLEASE EXCUSE HIM. I'LL HAVE TO TRANSLATE.>
SMILE, LARGO, OR YOUR WRIST WON'T BE THE ONLY THING I BREAK OFF.
GUAH!

<SO, HOW LONG HAVE YOU BEEN SEEING EACH OTHER?>
<NOT LONG, WE JUST MET A FEW WEEKS AGO.>
<HAYA-SAKA-SAN?>
<OH!>
<YES PIRO?>
<I... I HAVE TO GET BACK TO THE STORE.>
<PLEASE REMEMBER TO CALL NANASAWA-SAN. SHE REALLY NEEDS TO TALK TO YOU.>
<OK, I WILL.>
WHERE'S HE GOING? COWARD! WE NEED BACKUP!!
<LARGO JUST MOVED HERE, ACT-UALLY.>
LARGO, IF YOU DO ANYTHING STUPID RIGHT NOW, YOU WILL DIE PAINFULLY.
RIGHT. WE ARE IN DANGER. WE MUSTN'T BE SEEN AS A THREAT.
<HE DID? SO DOES LARGO-SAN LIKE LIVING IN JAPAN SO FAR?>
I HAVEN'T SEEN THIS WOMAN IN TWO YEARS, AND IT'S IMPORTANT TO ME THAT SHE THINKS I'M DOING OK.
NOW SMILE.
PLEASE.
I CAN'T FEEL MY FINGERS.
<HE SAYS THAT HE'S ENJOYING JAPAN VERY MUCH.>
<PIRO-SAN?>

<PIRO-KUN?>
<PIRO-KUN!!>
<YOU DON'T HAVE TO PLAY WITH ME, BUT YOU CAN TALK TO ME.>
TK
<...AND ONE SLICE OF PECAN PIE.>
<CAN I GET YOU TWO ANYTHING ELSE?>
<NO, THANK YOU.>
<SO, WHY ARE YOU SO DEPRESSED, PIRO-KUN?>
<DO YOU FEEL DOWN BECAUSE YOUR BEST FRIEND HAS STARTED DATING SOMEONE?>
<THAT CAN HAPPEN, ACCORDING TO MY DATA.>
<NO, NO, THAT'S NOT IT. IM ACTUALLY REALLY HAPPY TO SEE THEM TOGETHER. IN FACT I...>
<WELL... SINCE WHEN HAS LARGO EVER CARED ABOUT GIRLS?>
<I'M THE ONE WHO ALWAYS FANTASIZED ABOUT HAVING A RELATIONSHIP. I KNOW EVERY-THING THERE IS TO KNOW ABOUT THEM. I'M THE EXPERT, RIGHT?>
<BUT THERE HE IS, SOMEHOW DOING ALL THE RIGHT THINGS. HE HAS NO IDEA WHAT TO DO BUT HE'LL DO ANYTHING FOR HER.>
<THE BEST I CAN DO IS RUN AND FIND SOMEONE ELSE TO HELP THE GIRL I LIKE.>
<SOME EXPERT I TURNED OUT TO BE.>

<IF YOU REALIZE THIS, PIRO-KUN, WHY DON'T YOU DO SOMETHING ABOUT IT? YOU COULD START SMALL, YOU COULD CALL HER.>

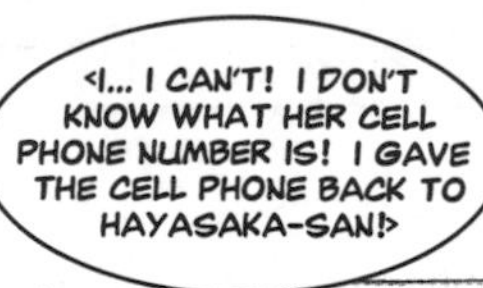
<I... I CAN'T! I DON'T KNOW WHAT HER CELL PHONE NUMBER IS! I GAVE THE CELL PHONE BACK TO HAYASAKA-SAN!>

<I'M SO STUPID. HER NUMBER WAS FLASHING RIGHT THERE ON THE SCREEN.>
<WHY DIDN'T I WRITE IT DOWN?>
<STUPID, STUPID.>

<NO, NO. I DID THE RIGHT THING. NANASAWA NEEDS TO TALK TO HAYASAKA-SAN, NOT ME. I CAN'T LET MY INTEREST IN HER MESS UP HER LIFE.>

<PIRO-KUN, STOP IT! YOU ARE NOT MESSING UP HER LIFE BY SHOWING INTEREST IN HER!!>

<WHAT IF SHE ACTUALLY LIKES YOU? WHAT IF SHE BECOMES SAD BECAUSE YOU **DIDN'T** TRY TO HELP HER?>

<ISN'T THAT MESSING UP HER LIFE TOO?>

<IF I GIVE YOU NANASAWA-SAN'S CELL PHONE NUMBER...>
<WILL YOU CALL HER?>

<YOU KNOW WHAT HER CELL NUMBER IS??>
<I HAVE VISUALS OF IT ON HAYASAKA-SAN'S CELL PHONE STILL CACHED IN MY MEMORY.>
<I AM A ROBOT, PIRO-KUN.>
<OH YEAH, I FORGET ABOUT THAT SOMETIMES.>
<YOU REALLY THINK I SHOULD CALL HER? WHAT IF SHE GETS MAD AT ME FOR FINDING HER CELL NUMBER?>
<THE LAST THING I WANT TO DO IS UPSET HER BEFORE HER RADIO SHOW TONIGHT-->
<ARE YOU AWARE THAT I HAVE FEELINGS FOR YOU, PIRO-KUN?>
<EH?>
<WHAT?>
<IF YOU CAN'T GRASP WHAT A FAKE GIRL WHO SEEMS REAL FEELS, HOW ARE YOU EVER GOING TO UNDERSTAND WHAT IS IN A REAL GIRL'S HEART?>
<I...>
<IF A REAL GIRL COMES INTO THE LIFE OF MY END USER, I'M PROGRAMED TO STEP ASIDE AND DISENGAGE THE EMOTIONAL STRINGS THAT ATTACH US.>
<I'M THEN SUPPOSED TO HELP MY END USER BUILD A "REAL" RELATIONSHIP.>
<I'LL GIVE YOU NANASAWA-SAN'S CELL NUMBER, PIRO-KUN.>
<BUT I WANT YOU TO DO SOME-THING...>
<FOR ME, TOO.>

<HAHAHA, OH DEAR!>
<PLEASE TELL LARGO-SAN THAT HE IS **VERY** FUNNY!>
<YES, HE CAN BE SOME-TIMES.>
FOOT... DAMAGED...
MUCH PAIN...
<WELL, I SHOULD LEAVE YOU TWO TO YOUR DATE.>
<IT WAS NICE TO MEET YOU, LARGO-SAN. BEST WISHES TO BOTH OF YOU!>
I DIDN'T SEE HER CIRCLE AROUND.
I THINK SHE IS GONE.
THAT WAS TERRIFYING. SELDOM HAVE I PH34RED LIKE THAT.
YOU PLAYED WITH GREAT SKILL.
DAMAGE WAS TAKEN, BUT WE MADE IT THROUGH.
JUNPEI WAS RIGHT.
LOV3 IS DANGER-OUS.
AHHH... MY FINGERS! I CAN FEEL THEM AGAIN!
EXCELLENT!
NOW TO SEE IF I CAN WALK.

七澤 希美子
090-9148-4498
<SO, ARE YOU GONNA CALL NANASAWA, OR JUST SIT THERE AND ADMIRE YOUR PHONE ALL EVENING?>
<GAH! HOW DID YOU-->
<YOUR PING-CHAN IS A CHATTY LITTLE THING.>
-CLICK-
<OH.>
<INTERESTING MACHINES, THESE E.D.S. UNITS.>
<SHE TOLD ME ABOUT HOW IN EXCHANGE FOR NANASAWA'S CELL NUMBER, YOU AGREED TO "PLAY" WITH HER, AND TAKE HER OUT ON SOME DATES.>
<SEEMS LIKE SHE'S REALLY EXCITED ABOUT GOING TO THIS "CAVE OF EVIL" THING TONIGHT.>
<YOU DO REALIZE I HAVE NANASAWA'S CELL NUMBER ON FILE. I WOULD HAVE GIVEN IT TO YOU IF YOU WANTED IT THAT BAD.>
<Y...YOU DO?>
WOOT!! CHECK THIS OUT!
14MS RESPONSE TIME, 1600X1200 NATIVE REZ, DVI INPUT, 700:1 CONTRAST RATIO...
T3H AWESOME! THAT'S BETTER THAN WHAT I SPEC'D!
MOST EXCELLENT.
YOU NOW HAVE EVERYTHING YOU NEED TO BUILD T3H MOST ULTIMATE BOX.
HEY, RELAX.
THESE COMPONENTS ARE TRULY L33T, BUT YOU N33D NOT PH34R THEM. YOU CAN HANDLE THEM.
ALL YOU HAVE TO DO IS PUT IT ALL TOGETHER.
MMM, ICE CUBES.
IF I SLEEP WITH YOU, WILL YOU GO AWAY?
crunch

thunk
I WILL NOT TAKE PART IN ANY SACRIFICIAL--
ENOUGH WITH THE CRAZY TALK!!
I NEVER WANTED YOUR HELP. I NEVER ASKED FOR YOU TO COME INTO MY LIFE.
I DON'T... WANT YOU HERE.
BUT YOU ARE. SO LET'S GET IT OVER WITH.
YOUR GAME AND YOUR RULES.
BUT IT DOESN'T MEAN I HAVE TO PLAY.
<OH DEAR. THE POOR THING REALLY ISN'T DOING ANY BETTER, IS SHE?>
GUAH!
<MYS--!>
<TUT TUT! I LEFT THAT NAME BEHIND LONG AGO... JUNPEI-SAN? IS IT?>
<JUNPEI WALLET!>
<MY MY, SUCH A HIGH LEVEL NINJA!>
<IT'S SO SAD. SHE DID A WONDERFUL JOB PLAYING A MAGICAL GIRL, BUT IN REAL LIFE SHE'S NOT VERY GOOD AT IT, IS SHE?>
<POOR LARGO-SAN.>
<YOU'D THINK THAT ERIKA HERSELF HAD TAKEN OUT THIS CONTRACT ON HIM.>
YEAH, WHATEVER.
I NEED A BEER.
SQUEEK!

<AH WELL. SHE IS A *PLAYSTATION* ACCESSORY.>
<MAKES SENSE THAT SHE'D WANT YOU TO PLAY WITH HER.>
I GUESS.

<OF COURSE, WITH REAL WOMEN, YOU NEVER KNOW IF THEY WANNA PLAY OR NOT.>

<FRIGGIN NUISANCE, REALLY.>
<BUT THAT'S JUST PART OF THE GAME.>

<SO PLAY ALREADY.>

UWAH!
-breeeep- -breeeep- -br

WHO... WHO'S NUMBER IS THAT?
ep- -breeeep-

<H...HELLO?>

<SO, PIRO-SAN, HAVE YOU CALLED HER YET?>

<OH, COME NOW. DON'T TELL ME YOU HAVEN'T CALLED HER YET.>
<I WAS JUST ABOUT TO WHEN YOU-->

<ARE YOU GOING TO LISTEN TO HER SHOW?>
<EH? UH, YEAH, OF COURSE.>
<DO YOU HAVE A RADIO?>
<PIRO-KUN! ARE YOU-->

<UH... I... I DON'T KNOW.>
AH~!
GANBATTE, PIRO-KUN!

<THERE HAS TO BE ONE AROUND HER SOME-WHERE.>
<I'M SURE BOSS-SAN-->
<I HAVE AN IDEA.>

<AFTER YOU CALL YOUR GIRL, WHY DON'T YOU AND PING COME DOWN TO THE "CAVE.">
<YOU CAN LISTEN TO MUMU'S RADIO SHOW IN KENJI'S OFFICE. HE HAS A WONDERFUL AUDIO SETUP UP THERE.>
<IN FACT, WE CAN RECORD IT FOR YOU.>

<YOU COULD GIVE HER A COPY. WOULDN'T THAT BE NICE?>
<UHM... MAYBE...>

<OH, BEFORE YOU COME, YOU MIGHT WANT TO CHECK ON YOUR FRIEND.>
<HUH? WHY?>
KTHUNK

<I THINK HE'S HAVING A BAD DAY, THE POOR THING.>
LET US SEE WHO IS KING OF THE IRON FIST!!
GAH!
-FWIP- THOOK!

WHAT ARE YOU DOING?? I WAS ON THE PHONE!
YOU GONNA PLAY OR YOU GONNA WHINE?
I STILL HAVE TO MAKE A--
HOOAH!! DOUBLE ARM FACE BUSTER!!
IN YOUR FACE!!
OWNED!!
WOOHYA!
TATATATATAT TATATATAT TATATATATAT
DAMNIT, DAMNIT DAMNIT! I'VE GOT TO MAKE THIS CALL!
IF I SCREW THIS UP I'LL NEVER FORGIVE--
MYSELF...
<UHM, BOSS-SAN? WHEN DID LARGO COME BACK?>
<A FEW HOURS AGO.>
<WAS HAYA-SAKA-SAN WITH HIM?>
<NOPE, HAVEN'T SEEN HER AT ALL TODAY.>
HM.
LARGO SEEMED DRUNK EVEN FOR LARGO.
I WONDER, DID SOME-THING...
OF COURSE SOMETHING HAPPENED. DUH.
BUT LARGO'S NOT THE TYPE WHO WOULD...
WOAH.

WOW, IT MUST HAVE BEEN BAD. I'VE NEVER SEEN HIM DRINK LIKE THIS BEFORE.
I WONDER IF HE'S OK. TALK ABOUT TRYING TO DRINK YOURSELF NUMB.
AAGHH!!
I DON'T HAVE TIME FOR LARGO'S PROBLEMS RIGHT NOW! I HAVE A CALL TO MAKE!
BIP!
eee. breee. bre
<HI~! THIS IS NANASAWA! PLEASE LEAVE A MESSAGE!>
CHIME!
BIP!
I WONDER IF LARGO HAS ANY BEER LEFT.

<MAKE IT QUICK, NANASAWA. WE CAN'T BE LATE TO THIS.>
<OK! I'LL BE QUICK!>
<TWO CALLS FROM... WHOSE NUMBER IS THAT?>
<HUH.>
<NO CALL FROM ERIKA.>
<SHE'S NOT ANSWERING HER PHONE. ISN'T SHE BACK YET?>
<HELLO, MEGA-GAMERS.>
<YANAGI-SAWA-SAN?>
<OH, HEY NANASAWA. READY FOR YOUR BIG RADIO DEBUT?>
<N...NO! NOT REALLY.>
<UHM...>
<IS PIRO-SAN THERE?>
<NOPE. HE LEFT A WHILE AGO. SAID SOMETHING ABOUT RECORDING YOUR SHOW SOME-WHERE.>
<OH.>
<HE DID?>
<YEAH, DIDN'T HE CALL YOU?>
<HE CALLED ME??>
<HE BETTER HAVE. HE SPENT THE WHOLE AFTERNOON IN THE BACK ROOM WORKIN' HIMSELF UP TO HIT THE "SEND" BUTTON.>
<THAT WAS HIS NUM-BER?>
<LORD. CHECK YOUR VOICE MAIL, GIRL.>
HAI.
<HE... DID! TWO VOICE MAILS!>
<NANASAWA, TIME'S UP, LETS GO.>

<...THEN ARE YOU UPSET BECAUSE LARGO-SAN SAT ON YOUR GLASSES AND BROKE THEM?>
<NO.>
<THEN ARE-->
<PING, PLEASE.>
<BUT, PIRO-SAN...>

<YOU'RE UPSET. WHAT'S WRONG?>

<IT'S NOTHING, PING.>
<I'M FINE.>

<HE'S NOT FINE. BASED ON HIS EVASIVE ANSWERS AND BEHAVIORAL CHANGES, I CAN ONLY BE A 72.3% SURE, BUT...>

<I THINK NANASAWA-SAN REJECTED HIM.>

<I CAN'T WAIT, PIRO-KUN! THIS IS GONNA BE SO MUCH FUN!>
<UHN.>

<YOU'LL DANCE WITH ME, WON'T YOU PIRO-KUN?>
<HUH? HUH?>

<UWAAAHHHHHH!!!>
<MATSUI-KUN!! YOU'RE MAKING THE POOR GIRL SAD AND GLOOMY WITH THAT DEPRESSING GAME YOU'RE MAKING HER WORK ON!!>
<IT'S NOT DEPRES-SING, MUMU-->
<JUST LOOK AT HER!!>
<I'M NOT GLOOMY, MUMU-SAN, REALLY! I-->
<LIFE IS ABOUT BEING HAPPY! NO SAD GIRLS ON MY SHOW!>
<LUCKILY, TODAY WE HAVE THE FABULOUS AND FAMOUS SHIGEO-SAN WITH US!>
<SHIGEO CAN MAKE ANY GIRL HAPPY WITH HIS GAMES!>
PAT PAT
<MUMU-CHAN, PLEASE...>
<MAKE HER HAPPY, SHIGEO-SAN!!>
<WE'RE ON IN 20!>
<LALALA LAAAA~!>
<I WISH MUMU WOULD TONE IT DOWN A NOTCH SOME-TIMES.>
<DON'T WE ALL?>
<MUMU IS BEING SILLY AS USUAL, BUT SHE'S RIGHT ABOUT ONE THING, YOU DO SEEM KINDA DOWN. ARE YOU OK?>
<EH? UHM, YES! I'M FINE! I'M JUST... A LITTLE NERVOUS.>
<I'M SORRY.>
<DON'T BE. YOU DON'T HAVE TO SAY ANYTHING PROFOUND. JUST RELAX AND BE YOURSELF.>
<I'LL KEEP MUMU FROM BEATING UP ON YOU TO MUCH.>
<UHM, THANK YOU, CHIBA-SAN.>
<SO, NANASAWA-SAN...>
<WHAT CAN I DO TO MAKE YOU HAPPY?>

<DOWN HERE, PIRO-KUN!>
<UN.>
CAVE OF EVIL
INTO THE DARKEST VOID.
LIKE A LAMER TO THE SLAUGHTER.
SQUEEK!
NO CROSSBOWS, NO CHAINSAWS, NO GRENADES, NOT EVEN A CROWBAR.
I'VE GOT NOTHING, BOO.
SQUEEK.
3NDRUN
THE FOOL IS ON HIS OWN.
SQUEEK?
IF WE BOTH DIE DOWN HERE, I'M GONNA BE PISSED.

<ISN'T THIS GREAT, PIRO-KUN!>
<UN.>

I TAKE IT YOUR LITTLE PHONE CALL DIDN'T GO WELL.

GUWAH!
<MIHO-CHAN! THIS PLACE FEELS SO MUCH MORE ALIVE WHEN IT'S FULL OF PEOPLE!>
<DOESN'T IT?>
H-HOW DID--

OH PIRO, PIRO, PIRO. LOOK AT HOW PING IS CLINGING TO YOU. IT'S PRETTY OBVIOUS THAT SHE'S SWITCHED TO REJECTION RECOVERY MODE.
REJECTION... WHAT?

BUT I--
YOU DON'T KNOW ANYTHING ABOUT PING, DO YOU?
E.D.S. UNITS ARE PROGRAMMED TO HELP THEIR END USERS LOSE THEIR FEAR OF REJECTION BY EASING THE PAIN OF IT WHEN IT HAPPENS.
THE IDEA IS THAT OVER TIME, IT BECOMES EASIER TO WORK UP THE COURAGE TO ASK GIRLS OUT, SINCE YOUR E.D.S. UNIT WILL TAKE CARE OF YOU IF THINGS DON'T GO WELL.

B... BUT I DIDN'T...
HMMM... I WONDER...
<UWAHH... I WISH I HAD AN ENGLISH MODULE!>

SHOULD I TRY TO DO THE SAME THING FOR LARGO? SHOULD I USE MYSELF TO TRY TO EASE HIS PAIN?

WEH? WHAT??

<HEY, TOHYA, THAT GUY YOU TOLD US TO KEEP AN EYE OUT FOR IS HERE. HE LOOKS TANKED.>

HELLO LARGO. FEELING ANY BETTER?
L-L-LARGO??
<LARGO-SAN!>
WHAT ARE YOU...
DID YOU FOLLOW ME HERE??
WE'RE GOING.
NOW.
WHAT? NO! I CAME HERE TO DO SOME-THING!
LIKE WHAT, DIE? YA DAMN IDIOT. LESSS' GO.
NO!
<PIRO-SAN?>
<YOU NEED TO HURRY OR YOU'LL MISS MUMU'S SHOW. KENJI SAYS HE'LL TAKE YOU UP TO HIS OFFICE AND GET YOU SET UP.>
I'LL KEEP AN EYE ON LARGO 'TILL YOU GET BACK.
PIRO!!
SHHHH...
DON'T WORRY. PIRO CAN TAKE CARE OF HIM-SELF.
AND IT WILL GIVE YOU AND I SOME TIME TO TALK.
TALK?
I'VE GOT NOTHIN' TO SAY TO YOU.
OH?
A WOMAN SHREDDED YOUR PRIDE TODAY...
AND I THINK YOU WANT TO TALK ABOUT IT.
WOULD YOU LIKE A DRINK?

<WALTAH...>
<SOME-THING OLD AND UNOPENED.>
<YES MISS.>
-thap-
-tap-
NOTE THE BOTTLE IS STILL SEALED.
ALSO, IT'S ALMOST OLDER THAN I AM. YOU CAN BE FAIRLY SURE I HAVEN'T TOYED WITH IT.
WHA'IS IT? 'SHOUSANDS OF YEARS OHLD?
LARGO, SIT DOWN BEFORE YOU FALL DOWN.
I WILL STAND, OR I WILL FALL.
I WILL NOT SIT.
<SO, YOU THINK MIHO-CHAN IS DOING OK?>
<OH YEAH. I HAVEN'T SEEN HER THIS PLAYFUL IN AGES, IF EVER.>
<IT'S NICE TO SEE HER MAKING FRIENDS RATHER THAN DRIVING PEOPLE OFF IN TERROR.>
<SHE'S A REAL TRIP SOME-TIMES.>
<ALMOST LOST HER A FEW YEARS AGO.>
<WE WORRY A LOT ABOUT HER AROUND HERE. SHE'S A GOOD GIRL.>

<...WHEN IT'S DONE, COME FIND ME AND WE'LL BURN SOME CD'S FROM THE D.A.T. TAPE.>
<OK.>

<...I JUST JUMP AROUND FOR JOYYY
<HAVE FUN.>

<...MUMU-CHAN'S VOICEVOICE PARADISE IS BROUGHT TO YOU TODAY BY SUNTORY BIG DRINK AND...>
KERCHACK

<HIHIHI--! MUMU-CHAN HERE! WELCOME TO MUMU-CHAN'S VOICEVOICE PARADISE!! JA JAAAN!>

<TODAY WE HAVE A LITTLE BIT OF OLD AND A LITTLE BIT OF NEW!!>

<OLD??>

<YES, SHIGEO-SAN! OLD! OLD OLD OLD!!>

<UWAH! YOU'RE GOING TO MAKE ME CRY, MUMU-SAN!>

<NONO, DON'T CRY!! WE STILL LOVE YOU!>
<HOW COULD WE NOT? CHIBA-SAN IS A VETERAN VOICE ACTOR WITH COUNTLESS ROLES THAT I'M TOO LAZY TO LIST. YOU'VE BEEN AROUND FOREVER!!>
<BUT I'M NOT OLD.>

<YES YOU ARE! YOU AREN'T YOUNG AND CUTE LIKE OUR NEXT GUES
<PING...>
<DO YOU THINK THAT-->

<HEY!>
<WHAT'D YOU TURN THE STEREO DOWN FOR?? NANA-SAWA WAS JUST-->

<PIRO-KUN...>
<I DON'T THINK YOU SHOULD LISTEN TO THE SHOW.>

<SO! NANASAWA-SAN! WELCOME TO THE SHOW~~!>
<I UNDERSTAND THAT YOU ARE FRESH FROM THE STUDIO AND YOU MIGHT EVEN STILL BE IN CHARACTER!!>
<WELL, UM... IT WAS A LOT OF FUN AND IT WAS ALSO HARD BECAUSE I REALLY TRIED TO DO MY BEST.>
<I'M VERY NEW TO ALL OF THIS SO I HOPE EVERYONE LIKES WHAT I'VE-->
<OIOIOIOI, WHAT ARE YOU, A ROBOT? WHAT'S WITH THE FAKE HAPPYHAPPY?>
<EH?? I... AH...>
<HMMM... EVEN SITTING NEXT TO SHIGEO-SAN ISN'T MAKING THIS GIRL GIDDY. THAT CAN MEAN ONLY ONE THING...>
<BOY TROUBLE~! YOU HAVE BOY TROUBLE!!>
<REHH??>
<HAH! I KNEW IT! THE MUMU SEES ALL!!>
<ACTUALLY, MUMU-CHAN, I THINK IT'S **FANBOY** TROUBLE!>
<EH?>
<THINK OF ALL THOSE OBSESSIVE SCARY FANBOYS THAT LISTEN TO YOUR SHOW.>
<OF COURSE IT'D MAKE A CUTE, GENTLE GIRL LIKE NANA-SAWA-SAN NERVOUS.>
<UWAAAAAH~!! YOU'RE SO RIGHT, SHIGEO-SAN! BUT IT'S SOMETHING SHE'LL HAVE TO GET USED TO~!>
<FANBOYS CAN BE SCARY AND CREEPY! ONE TIME I WAS IN AKIHABARA AND-->
<UHN HUH!>
<HEY.>
<HEY!!>
<HOW CAN YOU TALK ABOUT YOUR FANS THAT WAY??>
<THAT POOR FANBOY MIGHT BE LISTENING!!>

<UH, PING? WHAT ARE YOU DOING?>
<LET HER GO, PIRO-KUN.>
<I DON'T WANT TO SEE YOU GET HURT!>
<WHU...>
<WHAT THE HELL ARE YOU TALKING ABOUT??>
<EHHHH... YEAH, BUT NANASAWA-SAN, EVEN OTAKU MAKE FUN OF THEMSELVES FOR BEING SO PATHE-->
<THAT DOESN'T MEAN WE SHOULD TOO!>
<CAN YOU POSSIBLY UNDERSTAND WHAT IT'S LIKE TO FEEL THAT WAY ABOUT YOURSELF?>
<TO FEEL YOU HAVE LITTLE OR NO HOPE OF EVER HAVING A REAL GIRL IN YOUR LIFE? TO LIVE OFF OF THE FANTASIES CREATED AROUND GIRLS LIKE YOU AND ME JUST TO COPE?>
<EH, ER I-->
<THERE WILL BE OTHER GIRLS, PIRO-KUN.>
<GIRLS WHO UNDERSTAND YOU, GIRLS WHO WANT TO PLAY WITH YOU.>
<FOR NOW... PLAY WITH ME?>
<I'M NOT REAL. I CAN'T HURT YOU.>
<YOU DON'T HAVE TO BE AFRAID OF ME, PIRO.>
<I DON'T THINK FANBOYS ARE SAD AND PATHETIC. I THINK **WE** ARE BECAUSE WE CAN'T DO MORE FOR THEM EXCEPT SIT HERE AND TALK ABOUT HOW GREAT WE ARE WHILE THEY PRETEND WE ARE SOMEHOW PART OF THEIR LIVES.>
<AH HAH HAHAH... NANASAWA-SAN, CALM DOWN, CALM DOWN-->
<AND YOU.>
<WHEN WAS THE LAST TIME **YOU** WERE AFRAID TO CALL A GIRL YOU LIKED?>

<WHAT THE...!>
<D... DAMNIT... PING!>
<G... GET OFF OF ME!!>
<WHAT THE HELL ARE YOU DOING??>
<B...BUT PIRO-KUN! SHE REJECTED YOU! SHE-->
<SHE DIDN'T REJECT ME!!>
<I NEVER TALKED TO HER!!!>
<ABUH, UH WELL, THERE CAN BE TIMES, YEAH, UH, SOMETIMES YOU MEET A GIRL THAT MAKES YOU FEEL-->
<IF SHE DROPPED HINTS THE SIZE OF A COMMUTER TRAIN THAT SHE WANTED TO HEAR FROM YOU, WOULD YOU STILL BE TOO NERVOUS TO DIAL HER NUMBER?>
<WELL, NO, NOT TO DIAL-->
<RIGHT.>
<A LOT OF "FANBOYS" WOULD GIVE ALMOST ANYTHING TO HAVE THE KIND OF SELF CONFIDENCE YOU DO.>
<IT TOOK ME HOURS TO WORK UP THE GUTS TO DIAL HER NUMBER. THEN I COULDN'T EVEN LEAVE A FRIGGIN' MESSAGE!>
<ALL I EVER GOT WAS HER VOICE MAIL, AND WHEN I DID, I DIDN'T EVEN LEAVE A MESSAGE.>
<I REJECTED MYSELF, PING.>
<YOU CAN'T HELP ME WITH THAT.>
<EVEN I HAVE A LITTLE SELF CONFIDENCE. NOT A LOT, JUST A LITTLE.>
<SOME PEOPLE DON'T HAVE ANY. THEY DON'T BELIEVE IN THEMSELVES AT ALL.>
<THEY CLING TO OUR CHARACTERS BECAUSE THEY FEEL LIKE WE UNDERSTAND THEM.>
<MANY USE THE FANTASIES WE CREATE AS A BRIDGE BETWEEN THE REAL WORLD AND THEIR OWN TROUBLES AND FEARS.>
<WE MAY NOT SHARE THEIR PROBLEMS, BUT THEY NEED TO KNOW WE RESPECT THEIR STRUGGLES WITH THEM.>

SMALL SIPS, LARGO. SMALL SIPS.
DO NOT TELL ME HOW TO DRINK.
-GUAH-
YOU COULDAT LEAST USE A GLASS.
YOU REALLY ARE A BRUTE, AREN'T YOU.
NOT PLEASANT, IS IT?
NOT BEING ABLE TO GET AWAY FROM WHAT YOU FEEL INSIDE.
PAIN, FRUST-RATION,
LIFE...
WHAH YOU KNOW AHBOUT LIFE 'SEPT EATIN IT?
YEH UNDHEAD WHENCH...
"UNDEAD WENCH," AM I?
HEH.
BACK THEN...
WHEN WE PLAYED, AND I FINALLY MANAGED TO KILL YOU...
HOW DID IT MAKE YOU FEEL?
DIN'N CARE.
PLAY'D 'NOTHER GAME.
:crink:
BHALDURS GHATE. DEN SUPUR MUNKHEY BALL.
KHCK'D MUSH ASS... DIN'N CARE.
SO...
WHY IS THIS... ANY DIFFERENT?

IS IT BECAUSE IT'S REAL?
BECAUSE... SHE'S REAL?
REAL BREASTS...
SOFT LEGS...
WARM HIPS...
AND FLESH SHE WILL NEVER, **EVER** LET SOMEONE LIKE YOU TOUCH?
-FWUSH-
WOOM! WOOM! WOOM! WOOM! WOOM! WOOM! WOOM! WOOM! WOOM! WOOM!
PIRO!!
HE CAN'T HEAR YOU, LARGO.
'ERR GOIN.

GHETAWAY FRO' ME, YA UNDEAD--
UNDEAD?
ZOMBIE? VAMPIRE? WITCH? CREATURE OF THE DARK?
WHICH IS IT, LARGO?
IS THAT WHAT YOU THINK WHEN YOU LOOK AT ME??
THERE ARE ALL KINDS OF WAYS TO DIE, LARGO.
SOME PAINFUL...
SOME BITTER-SWEET.
YET SOME CAN LEAVE YOU WITH A BEATING HEART...
AND A WARM BODY.
SURPRISED, LARGO?
SURPRISED THAT I'M WARMER THAN YOU ARE?
AHH?
<HOW **DARE** YOU.>

<MESSING WITH HIM LIKE THAT WHEN HE'S SO DRUNK HE CAN'T EVEN STAND?>
<WHAT THE HELL IS WRONG WITH YOU??>
<I WAS WORRIED THAT LARGO WAS GONNA DO SOMETHING STUPID AND **YOU** MIGHT GET HURT. BUT WHAT DO I FIND? YOU PAWING HIM UP AND PLAYING SOME KIND OF SICK, TRAMPY MIND GAME ON HIM!>
<DO YOU HAVE ANY IDEA WHAT HE'S BEEN THROUGH TODAY? DO YOU EVEN KNOW WHY HE TRIED TO DRINK HIMSELF SENSE-LESS??>
<DO YOU EVEN CARE?>
I DIDN'T THINK SO.
COME ON, LARGO. LETS GO.
SH'GOH MEH PIRUH... SH'GOH MEH.
AHM DUHHN FURR...
SH'GOH MEH, PIRRRUH...

<P...PIRO-KUN?>
<M...MIHO-CHAN?>
<MIHO-CHAN IS UPSET. MIHO-CHAN NEEDS ME. PIRO-KUN IS UPSET. PIRO-KUN NEEDS ME.>
<MIHO-CHAN IS MY FRIEND. I CARE ABOUT MIHO-CHAN.>
<PIRO-KUN IS IMPORTANT TO ME. I CARE ABOUT PIRO-KUN.>
<PIRO-KUN CARES ABOUT ME. MIHO-CHAN CARES ABOUT ME.>
<MIHO-CHAN IS CRYING. MIHO-CHAN CARES ABOUT PIRO-KUN.
<PIRO-KUN NEEDS TO CARE ABOUT MIHO-CHAN!>
<PIRO-KUN!!>
<MIHO-CHAN?>

YKNOW, BETWEEN THE TWO OF YOU I DIDN'T GET TO HEAR ANY OF NANASAWA-SAN'S RADIO SHOW.
<YOU HEAR ME, PING?>
SH'GOH ME... SOH CHOLD...

<PING?>
WAITAMINUTE... DIDN'T SHE FOLLOW US OUT OF THE--
BHLOOD... DRAYNED...
CAN'T... FHEEL...

MUH BLOOHD!! I CHANT FHEEEL MUH BLOOD!!
OOF!

HAF I... BECOME ONE ODA LIV'N DHEAD ???
YOU'RE MAKING PROGRESS, IF THAT'S YOUR GOAL.

AH DUN WANNA 'COME A ZSHOMBI, PIRRUH!
LARGO...
WHAT HAPPENED BETWEEN YOU AND HAYASAKA-SAN TODAY?

HUYASA... HAYUSUS...?
ERIKA, LARGO. E-RI-KA.
THE GIRL WHO'S GOT YOU ACTING WEIRDER THAN USUAL?

ERI...
KA.
ERIKA.
ERIKA.

AH WILL NOT BECOME ON'ER YER UNDHEAD MHINIONS!! IF YA KILL MEH, Y'LL HAVE TO KHILL ME F'REAL!!!
AH AM AHLIVE!! AH WILL NOT SUFFA BE'N PAHLY DEAHD!!

OHH.
WHEAPON TRAILS.
PRETTY.
COMEON, LETS GET YOU HOME.

MY COMRADE RISKED CERTAIN DEATH TO PULL ME BACK FROM THE BOWELS OF HELL.
BUT WE AREN'T SAFE YET.
THUMP
THERE IS DEATH IN THESE STREETS...
FOLLOWING US...
WATCHING US...
WHAT A WONDERFUL DAY. I MISSED NANASAWA'S RADIO SHOW, I TOTALLY BOMBED CALLING HER, I LOST PING,
AND NOW I HAVE TO DRAG YOUR DRUNK ASS HOME.
YAY ME.
GURK!!
OW!! HEY--
-breeeeep-
TAK TAK
WHUMPH!
GREAT. THAT'S PROBABLY TOHYA.
SHE CAN TEAR INTO ME IF SHE WANTS TO, BUT IF PING IS THERE, SHE'S SENDING HER HOME RIGHT--
WEH?
N...N... NANASAWA?
CALLING...
ME?
-breeeeep- -breeeeep-
OH...
FSCK.

eeee - breeeee - breeeee - breeeee -
-CLICK-
<H... HELLO?>
<PIRO-SAN?>
<N... NANA-SAWA-SAN?>
<UH... HI! H... HOW ARE YOU?>
<I'M SO SORRY, I WAS IN THE STUDIO WHEN YOU TRIED TO CALL.>
<THAT'S OK! YOU WERE WORKING! I, UHM... I...>
<DID YOU...>
<DID YOU LISTEN TO THE RADIO SHOW?>
<YOU'R SHOW!>
<UHM, AH... I...>
UWAH!!
-OOF!-
RAHN!! PRRUH, WE GOHHAGEH AWWAH!!
LARGO, STOP IT, I'M ON THE--
THUD
-CRACKLE-
-FWUD-
WEH MUS FEE!!! DIS ENEMAH IS BEYONUS BOSH!!!
LARGO!!! WILL YOU STOP... OW!
NO, DON'T! <I'M SORRY MA'M!! PLEASE EXCUSE US!>
<AIEEEEE!!!>
NEED WHEPONZ!! NEEH
GAH!!! LARGO, NO!!
-CRASH-
<PIRO-SAN? WHAT'S WRONG?? IS THAT... LARGO-SAN?>
<YES!! SOMETHING HAPPENED BETWEEN HIM AND HAYASAKA-SAN, AND HE'S NOT TAKING IT VERY WELL.>
<EH? WITH... ERIKA??>
<HE'S TOTALLY HAMMERED, AND I'M HAVING TROUBLE-->
GAH!! LARGO, NO!
PANSS AREHINDER'N MEH!! DE MUS GO!!
PULL YOUR.... WHAT IS IT WITH YOU AND THE PANTS!
<AIEEEEE!!!>
SONNOVA....
GAH!!
<WHERE ARE YOU??>

IT IS OVER.
I HAVE LOST TOO MUCH BLOOD.
MY BODY FEELS LIKE LEAD.
I CANNOT MOVE.
WHY DOES SHE NOT ATTACK?
WHY DOES SHE WAIT?
IS SHE WAITING... FOR OTHERS?
ARE THERE MORE??
MORE... CIRCLING... AND WAITING...
WAITING...
...TO MAKE THE PERFECT KILL.
NO...

<POOR LARGO-SAN! YOU DON'T LOOK WELL AT ALL!>
<HE'S ALWAYS A PAIN WHEN HE'S TANKED, BUT HE'S NEVER BEEN **THIS** BAD BEFORE.>

<I'LL HELP YOU CARRY HIM. WE NEED TO GET HIM HOME.>
<NO, NO, THE WAY HE'S FLAILING AROUND, YOU MIGHT GET H-->

WHOCK!
EEE!
NUHHH!!!!!

<PIRO-SAN!!>
OW~! SONNOVA...

LARGO!!!
<ARE YOU OK?>
<PIRO-SAN?>

<AUGH...>
<GOTTA STOP HIM.>
<CAN'T LOSE HIM...>
<WOW... HE'S FAST.>

<NANASAWA?>
<WHAT ARE YOU... WAIT!!>

I CANNOT... BELIEVE... THE POWER...
DO THEY ALL POSSESS IT??
IS THERE NO ESCAPE??
ARE WE ALL DOOMED???
<PIRO-SAN?>
WHAT IS SHE DOING??
BHKH.
<NANA-SAWA!!!>
<SO NANA-SAWA-SAN'S HEART IS ENTWINED IN THIS TOO.>
<OH DEAR.>
<WHAT SHOULD I DO?>
<JUNPEI THINK YOU DO NOTHING.>
MOU~!
YAMETE KUDASAI, LARGO-SAN!!
DOOMED.
EVASIVE ACTION!!

SHITSUREISHI-MASHITA~!
I AM DAMAGED.
I AM WEAK.
<GOOD-NESS!>
<OH MY.>
<YOU **ARE** A PERSISTENT NINJA!>
<WHY WON'T YOU LET ME HELP THEM?>
I MUST FIND A SAFE PLACE.
I NEED TO HEAL.
NIGENAIDE KUDASAI, LARGO-SAN!!
OCHITSUITE KUDASAI YO~!
<JUNPEI KNOW WELL DEVASTATION CAUSED LAST TIME MYSTER-->
<SUCH A HANDSOME YOUNG MAN... WHY DO YOU NINJAS INSIST ON HIDING YOUR FACES?>
<JUNPEI MASK!!!>
I MUST GET AWAY.
I CANNOT HEAL IF I CANNOT GET AWAY.
TSUKAMAETA!

OH NO.
CRASH!!
EEK!
DAME!! ONEGAI DAKARA, NIGENAIDE KUDASAI!
ERIKA WA LARGO-SAN WO KIZUDUKERU TSUMORI JANAKATTA DESU YO!
TOO WEAK... IT'S OVER.
TSUMETAI NINGEN NI MIERU KAMO SHIRENAI KEDO, HONTOU WA KOKORO NO YASASHII KO DESU YO!
WHAT DOES SHE WANT?
WHAT IS SHE SAYING?
ERIKA WA NE, NANDOMO KIZUDUITE MOU NIDO TO HITO NI KOKORO WO HIRAKANAI TO OMOTTERUN DAKE DESU.
DEMO SORE WA TADA NO TSUYOGARI DESU. HONTOU WA ONAJI KOTO WO KURIKAESU NO WO TOTEMO KOWAGATTERU DESU YO, LARGO-SAN!
DEMO, ERIKA WA NE, KITTO LARGO-SAN NI AKIRAMETE HOSHIKUNAI TO OMOIMASU YO. SORE SINJITE-MASU!
I DON'T UNDERSTAND.
SHE'S NOT HURTING ME.
DAKARA, MOSHI ERIKA NO KOTO GA SUKOSHI DEMO SUKI DATTARA, AKIRAMENAIDE KUDASAI.
IT'S STRANGE...
AKIRAMEMASEN YO NE, LARGO-SAN. YAKUSOKO SHITE KUREMASU?
BUT I FEEL..
YAKUSOKU?
I FEEL...
URP

<OH DEAR.>
<L33T MASTER!!>
<POOR NANASAWA-SAN!>
<YOU DO REALIZE THAT I MAY HAVE BEEN ABLE TO PREVENT THAT.>
<BY ATTACK AND KILL L33T MASTER WHILE L33T MASTER NOT ABLE DEFEND SELF?>
<OHH... SO **THAT'S** WHAT YOU ARE SO WORRIED ABOUT.>
<WHY RETIRED MAGIC GIRL ACCEPT CONTRACT ON L33T MASTER?>
<WHY MYS... MISS TAKE ON SUCH JOB?>
<I HAVE MY REASONS. AS A MOTHER, AS A FRIEND, AND AS A MENTOR.>
<OH, RELAX, JUNPEI-SAN, DON'T BE SO TENSE! I CAN "NEUTRALIZE" LARGO-SAN AND HIS FRIEND SIMPLY BY TAKING THEM TO THE AIRPORT AND SHOOING THEM OUT OF THE COUNTRY!>
<BESIDES, I HAVEN'T EVEN DECIDED IF I'LL DO THAT YET.>
FHWIP!
<YOU NINJA ALWAYS THINK YOU HAVE TO KILL PEOPLE TO FIX THINGS.>
<NO WONDER YOU ARE ALL SO GLOOMY AND HIDE YOUR FACES BEHIND MASKS.>
TSK.

I CAN'T BELIEVE YOU THREW UP ON HER.
<OK, I'M BACK. SORRY THAT TOOK SO LONG.>
<NANASAWA-SAN, I AM SO SORRY ABOUT ALL OF THIS. I SHOULD NEVER-->
<PIRO-SAN, PLEASE! I TOLD YOU, IT'S OK! DON'T WORRY ABOUT IT!>
<HOW IS YOUR NOSE?>
<IT'S OK, I THINK.>
<I'M SO SORRY, LARGO HAS NEVER ACTUALLY GOTTEN SICK **ON** ANYONE BEFORE.>
<HEHEH.>
<THAT'S OK, THIS IS NOTHING COMPARED TO WHAT ERIKA USED TO PUT ME THROUGH.>
<E... HAYASAKA -SAN??>
<OH YEAH. I EVEN ENDED UP IN THE HOSPITAL ONCE.>
<WHA? YOU GOT HURT?>
<UH HUH.>
<HAVEN'T YOU EVER NOTICED?>
<NOTICED WHAT?>
<MY NOSE. IT'S CROOKED.>
<WELL, IT'S NOT REALLY ALL THAT NOTICEABLE, BUT...>
<ONE NIGHT WHEN ERIKA WAS REALLY DRUNK, SHE PUNCHED ME IN THE FACE AND BROKE MY NOSE.>
<IT NEVER REALLY HEALED QUITE RIGHT.>
<OH, DOES LARGO HAVE A RAIL CARD, OR DO WE NEED TO BUY HIM A TICKET?>
<LET'S SEE...>

<I'M GLAD LARGO-SAN FINALLY SETTLED DOWN.>
<YEAH, ME TOO.>
<UHM, NANASAWA-SAN?>
<ABOUT THE RADIO SHOW-->
<REEHHHH!! I'M SO SORRY, PIRO-SAN!>
<I DIDN'T MEAN TO TALK ABOUT YOU ON THE SHOW LIKE THAT!>
<PLEASE DON'T BE MAD!>
<EH? WHAT? HUH?>
<IT'S JUST THAT AFTER YANAGISAWA-SAN TOLD ME ABOUT HOW NERVOUS YOU WERE ABOUT CALLING ME, EVEN AFTER I SAID I WANTED TO TALK TO YOU, AND HOW YOU TRIED TWICE AND IN EACH VOICE MESSAGE I COULD HEAR YOU STRUGGLING FOR SOME-THING TO SAY AND THEN HANGING UP...>
<UGHEH!!>
<AND THEN, AS THEY SAT THERE, LAUGHING AT FANS, SAYING THEY ARE SCARY AND PATHETIC, IT JUST MADE ME SO MAD, BECAUSE... BECAUSE...>
<I THINK MOST OF THEM ARE A LOT LIKE YOU, AND DON'T DESERVE TO BE MADE FUN OF LIKE THAT, AND...>
<AND...>
<I'M SORRY...>
<I'LL... I'LL STOP TALKING NOW.>
LOHH, PIRR...
UP DEHR...
ISH DAT A POWWRRR UHP?

ISH IT A BAG OH AMMUH?
OHR BOMMZZ?
GAH!
LARGO! WILL YOU SIT...
...DOWN!
<NANASAWA-SAN, I NEVER GOT TO HEAR THE SHOW!>
OOF
BOMMZZ...
BOMZ GUD...
<YOU DIDN'T?>
<NO! BETWEEN LARGO AND PING AND...>
<EVERYTHING GOT SCREWED UP!>
<BUT... IF TALKING ABOUT ME HELPED YOU GET THROUGH THE SHOW...>
<THAT'S GOOD! I'M GLAD.>
<HEH. I STILL WISH I COULD HAVE HEARD IT. IF IT HELPED MAKE THE INTERVIEW A SUCCESS BY GIVING YOU SOMETHING-->
<NO!! IT WASN'T A SUCCESS! IT WAS A DISASTER!!>
<MUMU-SAN AND CHIBA-SAN JUST SAT THERE LAUGHING... AND... I COULDN'T HELP MYSELF. I... TORE INTO THEM.>
<I ACCUSED THEM OF BEING HORRIBLE PEOPLE. I SAID THE WORST THINGS.>
<I THINK...>
<I SCREWED UP.>
<YOU... DIDN'T SCREW UP, NANASAWA-SAN.>
<I DID.>

<YOU'RE BIG RADIO DEBUT GOT SCREWED UP BECAUSE I TRIED TO CALL YOU.>
<W... WHAT? NO!>
<IF I HADN'T CALLED, YOU WOULDN'T HAVE FELT SORRY FOR ME AND YOU WOULDN'T HAVE BEEN UPSET FOR YOUR SHOW.>
<PIRO-SAN, NOOO~ THAT'S NOT... I DIDN'T...>
<I NEVER SHOULD HAVE CALLED. I KNEW I'D SCREW THINGS UP FOR YOU. I KNEW IT!>
HNNN...
UGEH!
Y'RR BEIN PAHETIC.
SHTOP IT.
WHA? LET-- HOW WOULD YOU--
I C'N TELL.
'N YER MAKIN' 'ER CRY.
ALMOSH MAKE MEH CRY YUZZ SO PASHETIC.
Y'DAM LUSHER.
FIGHT TUH WHIN.
SHTOP FIGH'N LIKE A LUSHER.
'YER BETTER'N DAT.
YOYOGI... YOYOGI STATION. YOYOGI
SHEE'Z OK.
<LARGO-SAN, THE TRAIN IS STOPPING, YOU'LL-->
<AHH! LARGO-SAN!!>
-KTHUMP-

<ARE YOU SURE LARGO-SAN IS OK?>
<WELL, NO, BUT WE'LL SEE HOW FAR HE MAKES IT BEFORE WE HAVE TO CARRY HIM.>
<I KNOW FOR A FACT THAT HE'D RATHER CRAWL HOME THAN BE CARRIED HOME.>
<UH HUH, ERIKA IS THE SAME WAY.>
OU MAWAH, FOWWU BESHT!
<NEYOW!!> FFT!
<CAN YOU PLEASE STOP SAYING THAT?>
<UHH...>
<PIRO-SAN, I'M REALLY SORRY ABOUT MAKING YOU FEEL-->
<NO, NO, NO! DON'T WORRY ABOUT IT! IT'S NOT YOU! I'M FINE! I'M THE ONE WHO SHOULD BE APOLOGIZING TO YOU FOR...>
<FOR...>
<GEH.>
<EH?>
<WHY CAN'T I TALK TO YOU WITHOUT SOUNDING PATHETIC?>
<YOU DON'T SOUND PATHETIC!>
<YES I DO. I'VE WATCHED MORE THAN ENOUGH ANIME TO KNOW HOW TO SOUND LIKE A LOSER IN PERFECT JAPANESE.>
<YOU ARE NOT A LOSER, PIRO-SAN.>
<I DUNNO, I'M BEGINNING TO WONDER.>
<WHY DO YOU SAY THESE THINGS ABOUT YOURSELF?>

WHY DO I SAY SUCH THINGS...
<WHEN ERIKA'S LIFE FELL APART TWO YEARS AGO, SHE STARTED TO HATE HERSELF.>
<SHE FELT THAT EVERYTHING ABOUT HER WAS A LIE, AND THAT HER VERY EXISTENCE WAS A BURDEN TO EVERY-ONE WHO CARED ABOUT HER.>
<STUPID, ISN'T IT? THAT SOMEONE LIKE ERIKA COULD FEEL THAT WAY ABOUT HERSELF?>
<UHN.>
<DO YOU WANT ME TO GO AWAY, PIRO-SAN?>
<EH?? WHAT? NO! WHY WOULD YOU THINK THAT??>
<WHEN PEOPLE HURT THEMSELVES, THEY HURT THE PEOPLE THAT CARE ABOUT THEM.>
<ERIKA USED SELF HATRED TO TRY TO DRIVE AWAY THE PEOPLE WHO CARED ABOUT HER.>
<I'VE ALREADY HAD MY NOSE BROKEN ONCE, PIRO-SAN.>
<BUH....NANA-SAWA-SAN, I'D NEVER EVER-->
<KIMIKO.>
<WHA?>
<IT'S KIMIKO, PIRO-SAN.>

KIMIKO...
SAN?
<SO, WHAT HAPPENED TO YOUR GLASSES?>
<MY GLASSES?>
<OH, LARGO SAT ON THEM.>
<REHH? HE DID? HOW DID THAT HAPPEN?>
<WELL, IT'S MY FAULT, REALLY. I PUT THEM DOWN ON THE COUCH IN THE BACK ROOM.>
<CAN YOU SEE OK WITHOUT THEM?>
<WELL ENOUGH, I GUESS. I CAN SEE YOU OK, BUT THINGS START TO GET FUZZY WHERE LARGO IS.>
<THATS BETTER THAN ME, I'M BLIND WITHOUT MY CONTACTS.>
<YOU WEAR CONTACTS?>
SEE, BOO? YOU WORRY TOO MUCH.
SOMETIMES IT'S OK TO JUST LET THINGS HAPPEN.
EVEN YOUR MOST DIFFICULT CLIENTS CAN SURPRISE YOU.
I THINK OUR CLIENTS DID PRETTY GOOD TODAY.
I REALLY DO.
OOPS. SPOKE TOO SOON.
SQUEEK!!
WELL, AT LEAST FALLING HEAD FIRST INTO A DUMPSTER ISN'T REALLY A MORAL DILEMMA.

<NO, I HAVE NO IDEA WHERE SHE IS.>
<SHE SAID SHE WAS GOIN' TO THE LITTLE GIRL'S ROOM BUT NEVER CAME BACK.>
<NO, SHE'S NOT ANSWERING HER PHONE.>
<WHAT DO YOU MEAN IT WASN'T A TOTAL DISASTER? I'M GONNA HAVE A HEART ATTACK HERE!>
<I KNOW, MUMU IS A PRO, SHE RAN WITH IT. THAT DOESN'T MATTER, I GOTTA GET NANASAWA BACK HERE SO SHE CAN APOLOGIZE.>
<YEAH, YEAH, I KNOW SHE APOLOGIZED TO BOTH OF THEM ON THE SHOW, BUT SHE'S GONNA HAVE TO DO MORE THAN THAT.>
<OH HELL. MUMU'S HERE. I GOTTA DO SOME DAMAGE CONTROL. I'LL CALL YOU LATER.>
<MUMU-CHAN! HEY, SAYURI-SAN, WAS SAYIN' THAT THIS WAS THE FIRST TIME A GUEST HAS EVER LEFT YOU SPEECHLESS ON YOUR SHOW!>
<NO ONE EVEN THOUGHT THAT WAS POSSIBLE!>
<HEH, HEHEH...>
<HEH...>
<OH BOY. UH... LOOK, I REALLY HAD NO IDEA NANASAWA WAS GONNA DO THAT. SHE'S ALWAYS BEEN SO QUIET AND RESERVED AND STUFF, I...>
<UH...>
<HAAA~ HAHAHAH HAHAHAHAHA HAHAHAH!!>
WHAP WHAP WHAP
<HEEE HEEE...>
<I LIKE HER.>
<BRING HER BACK NEXT WEEK.>

<I'M HOME~!>
<WAHH... WHAT'S WITH ALL THE BAGS AND BOXES?>

<ERIKA?>

-FWIP!-

<WOW, WHAT A DAY.>
<HOW WAS YOURS? ANYTHING INTERESTING HAPPEN?>

<QUIET DAY, HUH?>

<REHHH... I CAN'T BELIEVE HOW OUT OF SHAPE I AM. I REALLY SHOULDN'T HAVE DONE THAT WITHOUT STRETCHING FIRST.>
FUMP!

<OH WELL...>
<BOY, IT'S BEEN **YEARS** SINCE I'VE BEEN TO A LOVE HOTEL.>

<WHAT?>
<YOU...>
<WHEN DID...>
<I DON'T KNOW WHAT YOU SAID TO LARGO-SAN, BUT HE TOOK IT PRETTY HARD.>
<YET I DON'T THINK HE'S GIVEN UP ON YOU YET. HE SEEMS KINDA STUBBORN.>
<YOU WANT ME TO TALK TO HIM TOMORROW? MAKE IT CLEAR YOU AREN'T INTERESTED?>
<MAKE HIM GO AWAY?>
<STOP IT, YOUR FACE IS GONNA GET ALL WRINKLY.>
<YOU DON'T WANT TO **SCARE** HIM AWAY, DO YOU?>
<NO...>
<UHM... NANA-SAWA...>
<YOU AND PIRO... DIDN'T REALLY...>
<HEHEH, NO, NO... I HAVEN'T BEEN TO A LOVE HOTEL SINCE YOU BUSTED ME IN THE FACE FOR DRAGGING YOUR DRUNK BUTT OUT OF ONE.>
<MMM... ACTUALLY, YOU HAVE.>
<TWICE THAT I KNOW OF.>
<REHHH??? TWICE??>
<ONCE.>
<MAYBE.>

<OH, HEY MOM. YOU'RE BACK.>
<DAD'S BEEN TRYING TO GET A HOLD OF YOU ALL EVENING.>
<OH DEAR, HAS HE?>
<YEAH, HE'S SULKING IN THE LIVING ROOM.>
<YOUR FATHER CAN BE SO SILLY SOME-TIMES.>
<SO, YUKI, HOW WAS YOUR DAY? ARE YOU FEELING ANY BETTER?>
<OH, YEAH, I AM.>
<MUCH BETTER.>
<IT WAS A GOOD DAY.>
<HEY, YUUJI, I'M DONE. YOU CAN USE THE BATH N-->
BAM!
<W... W... WHAT ARE YOU DOING???>
<WOAH.>
<INCOMING. WHAT NOW?>
<WHY DO YOU HAVE PICTURES OF THIS WOMAN ON YOUR SCREEN???>
END - CHAPTER 6

Megatokyo
leave it to seraphim!
Earth Friendly Fashions!
IN TODAY'S "SERAPHIM CHECK," WE'RE GOING EARTH FRIENDLY!
I HAVE DISCOVERED THAT CONVENTIONAL GROWN COTTON REQUIRES EXCESSIVE AMOUNTS OF PESTICIDES, HERBICIDES, FERTILIZERS, AND WATER AND IT DEPLETES THE SOIL.
IT'S ALL ABOUT ME.
TO EASE THE BURDEN ON THE EARTH, WE HERE AT MEGATOKYO WILL SOON BE EXPERIMENTING WITH MORE ECO-FRIENDLY, SUSTAINABLE FASHION TEXTILES!
LETS TAKE A LOOK AT SOME OF THE IDEAS WE'VE BEEN LOOKING AT.
SNAP
THIS SEXY NUMBER IS MADE FROM A SODA BOTTLE!
DID YOU KNOW THAT POLAR FLEECE CAN BE MADE FROM RECYCLED SODA BOTTLES?
THIS DRESS IS MADE ENTIRELY OF JUNK MAIL!
ORIGAMI SKILLS CAN BE HANDY!
AMERICANS GET ALMOST 4 MILLION TONS OF JUNK MAIL EVERY YEAR. THAT COULD CLOTHE A LOT OF PEOPLE!
NO!! FORGET IT! FUR IS NOT ECO-FRIENDLY!
IT ISN'T FRIENDLY, PERIOD!
SQUERK.
THIS IS BY FAR MY FAVORITE "SUSTAINABLE" OUTFIT!
100% NATURAL, BIODEGRADABLE, AND YOU CAN MAKE IT YOURSELF!
OF COURSE, YOU HAVE TO GO TO THE TROPICS TO MAKE ONE...
NOT LIKE THERE IS ANYTHING WRONG WITH THAT!!

Eigo_de_itte_kudasai.txt

<Hi~~! Nanasawa Kimiko here! How are you?>

<Things sure got messed up in the last chapter, didn't they? Largo-san seemed so upset that I was sure Erika had said some horrible things to him that she didn't really mean. I tried to talk to him and calm him down. I knew he couldn't understand me, but I think he understood what I was trying to say.>

<Piro-san tells me that many of you did not understand what I said to Largo-san on page 174. Well, duh! Neither did Largo-san! Most of the time, we translate our Japanese into English so you can understand what we are saying, but for this episode we decided that it would be better if you were to see and understand things from Largo-san's point of view. Difficult, isn't it?>

<Since you aren't SUPPOSED to understand what I said, you really don't need a translation, but Piro-san said we should post one for readers really want to know.>

<So stop now if you want to know only what Largo-san knows!>

-- FRAME 02 --

dame!! onegai dakara, nigenaide kudasai! erika wa largo-san wo kizudukeru tsumori janakattadesu yo!

<No!!! Please don't run away! Erika didn't mean to hurt you!>

-- FRAME 03 --

tsumetai ningen ni mieru kamo shirenai kedo, hontou wa kokoro no yasashii ko desu yo! erika wa ne, nandomo kizuduite mou nido to hito ni kokoro wo hirakanai to omotterun dake desu.

<She may seem cold, but she really is a caring person. Erika has been hurt so many times that she doesn't want to open up to anyone again.>

Eigo_de_itte_kudasai.txt

-- FRAME 04 --

demo sore wa tada no tsuyogari desu. hontou wa onaji koto wo kurikaesu no wo totemo kowagatteru desu yo, largo-san!

<But that is just a facade. She's really just so afraid of getting hurt again, Largo-san!>

demo, erika wa ne, kitto largo-san ni akiramete hoshikunai to omoimasu yo. sore sinjite-masu!

<But I think that Erika doesn't want you to give up on her. I believe that!>

-- frame 05 --

dakara, moshi erika no koto ga sukoshi demo suki dattara, akiramenaide kudasai.

<So, if you like her even just one bit, please don't give up on her.>

akiramemasen yo ne, largo-san. yakusoko shite kuremasu?

<You won't give up, right, Largo-san? Will you promise me that?>

-- frame 06 --

yakusoku?

<Promise?>

-- END --

<Piro-san told me I could go on for three more pages if I wanted to (something about really icky comics that could go away) but I think this should just about do it!>

<kimiko>

<PS: a big thank you to Eileen "Kaki" Hu for her help with my Japanese!!>

THEY ARE MINE! YOU CANNOT HAVE THEM!!
tak
tak tak

STORY & ART ≠ FRED GALLAGHER
HERBS AND SPICES - DOMINIC NGUYEN

AND NOW, A BRIEF MESSAGE FROM SHIRT GUY DOM.
SO, BECAUSE OF MY RANT LAST MONDAY, I'VE APPARENTLY EARNED A REPUTATION AS THE KING OF GAME AND ANIME PORN.

THIS WAS A REPUTATION I'D HAD BEFORE, MIND YOU, BUT AFTER THAT RANT, IT'S STARTED CREEPING INTO ALL AREAS OF MY LIFE, BOTH ONLINE AND IN PERSON.

HEY, GUYS! HOPE I'M NOT TOO LATE.

GUYS, THE PORN KING MADE IT!

YO, PORN KING, 'SUP?

...I HATE YOU ALL.

San Jose, CA
March 26, 2005

IT'S GOTTEN KIND OF ANNOYING, BUT I CAN LIVE WITH MOST OF IT.
HEY, DOM, THANKS FOR THE RIDE.
NOT A PROB, THE CD CASE IS UNDER YOUR FEET, PUT IN WHATEVER YOU WANT.
WHICH ONES ARE THE PORN MUSIC?
(THE SGDMOBILE)

Redwood City, CA
March 23, 2005

... ...
... --- ...
THEY'RE IN THE BACK.
WOOT!

BUT THE TITLE DOES HAVE ITS DOWNSIDE.
COOL, SEE YOU GUYS WHEN YOU GET HERE.
DAMN IT, STOP CALLING ME THAT!
OKAY, FINE, BE THAT WAY. I DON'T CARE.
BUNCHA KIDS, I SWEAR.
CLICK
RING *RING*
OH, FOR GOD'S SAKE, PEOPLE.

Sunnyvale, CA
March 25, 2005

YES, DAMMIT, YOU'VE REACHED THE PORN KING. THAT'S WHAT YOU WANTED TO HEAR, RIGHT?
LORD OF PORN, THAT'S ME!
THERE, I SAID IT, YOU LITTLE PACK OF...

A REALLY BIG DOWNSIDE.
OH.
HI, MOM.

Somewhere in Michigan
9 PM Eastern Time
HELLO? OH, HI DOM.
YEAH, THE NEXT CHAPTER IS SHAPING UP PRETTY NICELY. I CAN'T COMPLAIN TOO MUCH, FOR ONCE.
WHAT? I DON'T QUITE UNDERSTAND WHAT YOU'RE TRYING TO SAY.
(FRED'S EVIL GOATEE)
(FRED'S EVIL CABLE-EATING CAT)

Somewhere in California
6 PM Pacific Time
I SAID, THE WORD IS "CROSSOVER."
IF WE REALLY WANT MT TO GROW, WE NEED TO HAVE AT LEAST ONE GOOD CROSSOVER!
"WORLD'S FINEST" MADE BATMAN AND SUPERMAN THE PREMIER TEAM IN COMICS WORLDWIDE.
(ONE OF THE HAIRLESS FOLK)
(DOM'S EVIL HEAT-MONKEY LAPTOP)

IT'S NOT JUST SUPERHERO COMICS, EITHER! OTHER WEBCOMICS CROSS OVER ALL THE TIME, ESPECIALLY TO INSULT EACH OTHER!

SHOUNEN JUMP HAS HAD ITS SHARE OF CHARACTERS JUMPING INTO OTHER WORK TOO, LIKE WHEN YU-GI-OH! AND BOBOBOBO BOOBOBO CROSSED OVER!*

AND WHO CAN EVER FORGET THE MOST GENRE-BUSTING CROSSOVER OF ALL TIME?**

THE PUNISHER
MEETS
ARCHIE

JUST IMAGINE THE POSSIBILITIES! RENT-A-ZILLA VS. GODZILLA!
(I MEAN, GODZILLA WILL FIGHT ANYTHING IF YOU GIVE HIM ENOUGH MONEY!)
SWEET!
(LARGO)
(GODZILLA)
RAR!
(TOKYO)
(RAYMOND BURR)

WE COULD DOCUMENT MY ADVENTURES WITH THE REAL LIFE COMICS CREW!
(THEN I COULD STEAL GREG'S CAPCOM VS. EVERYTHING GAG)
THERE IS NO PEE IN ME! I HAVE PEED IT ALL OUT!
HOLY !$#%, I CAN SEE YOUR AURA!
NO LUBE FOR ME! WE OF THE HAIRLESS FOLK COME PRE-GREASED!
(SOUTHERN COMFORT)
(RUM WITH A SPLASH OF COKE)
GREG DEAN: DRUNK
CLIFF HICKS: DEAD DRUNK
DOMINIC NGUYEN: NO SUCH EXCUSE

JUST ONE OR TWO OF THESE, AND WE'D BE SET FOR LIFE!
SO, WHAT DO YOU THINK?
WELL, DOM, JUST ONE PROBLEM...

WE'D BE WRITING IT. THINK ABOUT IT.
...
...

UM, WHAT ABOUT CROSSING OVER WITH THE X-MEN? THEY'RE USED TO GOING NOWHERE FOR YE...
GIVE IT UP, DOM.

*YES, THIS ACTUALLY HAPPENED
**I'M NOT MAKING THIS ONE UP, EITHER.

そのころ。。。

a megatokyo moment

(THE MANAGEMENT REALLY WISHES IT COULD SACK THOSE RESPONSIBLE FOR THIS LAME COMIC.)

"DOM SINGS BARRY'"

I DO THE THINGS THAT MAKE THE WHOLE WORLD SCREAM~!
I WREAK THE HAVOC AND CHAOS AND EVERY-THING!
MICRO-PHONE
DOM

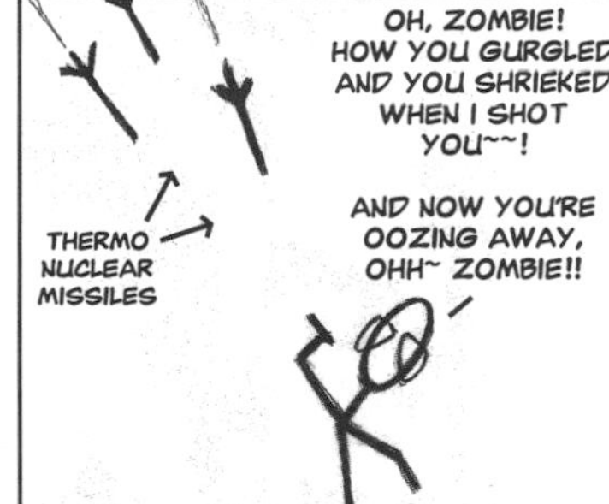

OH, ZOMBIE! HOW YOU GURGLED AND YOU SHRIEKED WHEN I SHOT YOU~~!
AND NOW YOU'RE OOZING AWAY, OHH~ ZOMBIE!!
THERMO NUCLEAR MISSILES

FOOM!
PARTS OF DOM
MORE PARTS

<PIRO> SO, WHADDYA THINK?
<DOM> ...
<DOM> I KNOW WHERE YOU LIVE. NO JURY ALIVE WOULD CONVICT ME.
<PIRO> OH, COME ON, IT'S CUTE.
A COOKIE

あいだに。。。

a megatokyo moment

"A WISH FOR ROCKETS THAT WORK."

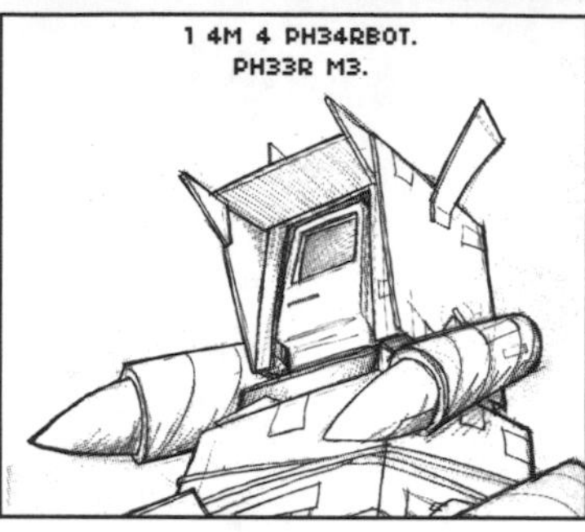
1 4M 4 PH34RBOT.
PH33R M3.

1 4M T3h SL33PI_3S PH34R.
MY V1GIL4NC3, 4 51L3N7 7HR34T,
MY W34PONZ, 4 H41L OF D347H.
<WHAT IS IT?>
<I DUNNO. LET'S KNOCK IT OVER.>
PH34R BOT

7HR347 D3T3CT3D.
3NG4G3 D3F--

WAH!!

<KAY!>

<WOOT!>

WHOMPH

THAT COULD
HAVE GONE
BETTER.

LOOKS LIKE SOMEONE FINALLY MANAGED TO FORWARD OUR MAIL TO US.
WOOT! ANYTHING GOOD?
WELL, LETS SEE. IT SEEMS THAT I'VE PERSONALLY CAUSED SEVERE FINANCIAL DAMAGE TO THE RECORDING INDUSTRY, SO THE *RIAA* IS SUING ME FOR $534,950.
HERE'S A BILL FOR $34,950 FROM *THE SCO GROUP* FOR RUNNING LINUX ON 50 SINGLE PROCESSOR MACHINES THEY THINK I HAVE.
AND... WHAT THE? *CLARIA* IS SUING ME FOR CALLING GATOR "*SPYWARE*' IN MY BLOG?!?
HAH HA! LITTLE DO THEY KNOW THAT I HAVE LINUX RUNNING ON OVER **100** MACHINES! MANY OF THEM HAVE DUAL PROCESSORS!! SOME EVEN HAVE **THREE** PROCESSORS!!

"WE IMMEDIATELY INSIST THAT YOU CHANGE REFERENCES FROM '*SPYWARE* TO EITHER '*EULA AWARE WARE* OR '*HAPPYWARE*'"??
CRAP. ANOTHER CEASE AND DESIST LETTER FROM *MICROSOFT*. THEY WANT ME TO STOP CALLING THE LARGO DESKTOP ENVIRONMENT "*LARDOWS*."
JURY DUTY.
OH, LOOK! A PACKAGE FROM THE US GOVERNMENT! I WONDER WHAT THIS COULD BE?
ARE WE SURE WE WANT TO GO BACK HOME?
DUDE, WE HAVE TO STICK THESE *RFID* TAGS SOMEWHERE ON OUR BODIES. SOMEHOW, THEY ARE SUPPOSED TO PROTECT US FROM EVIL.

I THINK WE ARE LOST. IF YOU LOOK HERE ON THE MAP...
ZOUNDS!! A WOODLAND CREATURE!!!
THERE SHOULD BE SOME SORT OF TOWN HERE.
SQUEE!!
WHACK!
WHACK!
WHACK!
-CRUNCH
-SPARKLE
BEHOLD! LOOK UPON WHAT I HAVE KILLED!
A VISCIOUS SPARKLE BUNNY!!!
THAT'S NICE.
NOW CAN YOU AT LEAST PRETEND TO HELP ME?
AS I WAS SAYING, EITHER THIS MAP IS WRONG, OR WE ARE REALLY LOST.
CHING!
-CRASH-
.THUMPH.
SQUISH!
I KNOW NOT WHAT THIS IS, BUT I KILLED IT ANYWAY!
PLEASE DON'T WAVE DEAD THINGS IN MY FACE, OR I'LL HURT YOU.
EVEN IF THE TOWN WAS ABANDONED, WE SHOULD STILL SEE TRACES OF IT.
WHACK
WHUMP
WHACK
WHUMP
AH! AND THERE! THE DREADED 3VIL 3GGPL4NT!
IT PUT UP A VALIANT STRUGGLE!!
LARGO. WE ARE TRYING TO GET THROUGH THIS FOREST, NOT DEPOPULATE IT.
CRACK!
CRACK!
CRACK
SNAP!!
BEHOLD! I HAVE FOUND SOME STICKS! I HAVE BROKEN THEM IN HALF!
I SHALL NOW SHARPEN THEM!!
I REALLY DON'T KNOW WHY I DON'T JUST SET YOU ON FIRE.

SHALL I...

STEP ASIDE, W3NCH.

YES!!

SKRUTCH!!

WOW! I HIT IT AS HARD AS I COULD AND DIDN'T DO ANY DAMAGE AT ALL!

YOU GUYS JUST... WOW!!

SINCE WE ATTACKED AS A GROUP, WE SHARE THE EXPERIENCE POINTS, RIGHT?

THIS IS SO COOL! I CAN'T WAIT TO LEVEL UP AGAIN!

WHEN I WOKE UP THIS MORNING, IT WAS A **BEAUTIFUL** DAY!!
THE SUN WAS SHINING! THE BIRDS WERE SINGING! I DECIDED THAT I WAS GOING TO MAKE TODAY A **GREAT** DAY!!
I WASN'T GOING TO LET ANYTHING RUIN IT! IT WAS GOING TO BE **MY** DAY!!
BUT IT **WASN'T** DESTINED TO BE MY DAY. THE CLOUDS ROLLED IN AND NEGATIVITY POURED DOWN ON ME LIKE A DRIVING RAIN, WASHING AWAY ALL MY HOPES AND DREAMS.
I WAS LEFT DRENCHED, COLD, EMPTY -- A LIFELESS SHELL. THE ONLY REASON I SEEMED TO EXIST WAS TO SUFFER, AND TO SUFFER... **ALONE.**

IT WILL **NEVER** BE **MY** DAY!! WHY, WHY MUST LIFE BE THIS WAY? WHY EVEN GIVE ME HOPE, WHEN IT IS ALWAYS, ALWAYS RIPPED AWAY??
IS THE RIPPING AWAY OF HOPE, DAY AFTER DAY, DESTINED TO BE PART OF MY SUFFERING??
OH, UNHAPPY LIFE!!!

P...PLEASE STOP READING RANDOM LIVE JOURNALS OUT LOUD.
IT'S... DAMAGING MY BRAIN.
OH, YOU'RE JUST JEALOUS THAT THEY ARE BETTER WHINERS THAN YOU ARE.

The Adventures of Piro & Seraphim:
adventures in running your own business
RUNNING YOUR OWN BUSINESS CAN BE A LOT OF FUN, BUT THERE CAN ALSO BE A LOT OF PROBLEMS.
SO WHEN DO WE GET TO THE "FUN" STUFF?
HUSH.
PROPERTY OF CEA
FOR EXAMPLE, WE'VE HAD NO END OF TROUBLE WITH THE SHOPPING CART SOFTWARE.
THE SITE IS DOWN AGAIN?*
WHAT BROKE THIS TIME??
DON'T ASK ME. YOU'RE THE ONE WHO PICKED THIS SOFTWARE.
*ACTUALLY HAPPENS. WE'RE REPLACING THE CART SOFTWARE THIS WEEK.
404
SOMETIMES THINGS DON'T COME OUT EXACTLY THE WAY YOU EXPECT THEM TO.
UHM... IS THE BEAR SUPPOSED TO BE DAY-GLOW ORANGE?*
MAYBE HE'S A RADIO-ACTIVE BEAR?
SO... THAT'D MAKE HIM A "HALF-LIFE" B34R?
*ACTUALLY HAPPENED. THE SHIRT PRINTER REPRINTED THE ORDER.
OF COURSE, MANUFACTURING STUFF YOURSELF DOESN'T MEAN THINGS WILL COME OUT EXACTLY RIGHT EITHER.
PIRO!! GET OUT HERE!!!
THE MUG PRESS IS ON FIRE!!!!*
*ACTUALLY IT STARTED SMOKING, AND PIRO WAS USING IT AT THE TIME.
(NOT LISTENING. HAS HEAD-PHONES ON.)
THEN THERE ARE ALL THE OFFICE MACHINES THAT NEVER SEEM TO WORK RIGHT.
SERA!! THE FAX MACHINE IS POSSESSED AGAIN!*
IT'S GROWLING AND THROWING THINGS AT ME!!
*HAPPENS OFTEN. PIRO IS THE ONE WHO BOUGHT THE FAX MACHINE.
RAWR! SQUEEEL!
(NOT LISTENING. NOT HER PROBLEM.)
THEN THERE ARE ALL THE OTHER LITTLE PROBLEMS...
PIRO, THE TOILET IS BROKEN.
AGAIN.
*ACTUALLY, IT IS HIS PROBLEM.
hisssssssss
(NOT LISTENING. PRETENDS IT'S NOT HIS PROBLEM.*)
YEAH, RIGHT.

SORRY...

PIRO AND SERAPHIM
RAN AWAY.

(WE'LL LET YOU KNOW
WHEN WE FIND
THEM.)

Dead_Piro_Art_Days.txt

"Dead Piro Days" happen when I post a single drawing or illustration rather than a whole comic. Since each *Megatokyo* comic takes from 8 to 14 hours to complete (yes, they are taking longer to do these days), every once and a while I get a little overwhelmed and have to miss a comic. DPDs are a way to give the readers something to look at on those days.

Even though most readers are never happy about the missed comics, DPDs themselves tend to offer interesting insights into the characters and the *Megatokyo* world. They are often used by people trying to gain a better understanding of the story.

Some of the best drawings I've done are DPD drawings. They are more purely intuitive pieces, usually following some creative whim that I happen to be on at the time. My brain can be quite annoying and sometimes will move off onto other ideas while I am still in the midst of producing comics based on earlier ones.

Sometimes DPDs are samples of what I might be working on other than the comic itself. Several of these DPDs are samples of work I was doing for Volume 3. In fact, for this book I did a series of DPD drawings that were literally part of the development process I went through in rewriting the "Circuity" story at the end of this book.

I think DPDs would be missed if I were to become so efficient that I never missed comics. Luckily, I don't think people have to worry about that, because I really don't see that ever, ever happening.

WHAT ARE YOU DOING?
I HAVE KILLED MANY THINGS. WE WILL NOW EAT THEM.
ONE CANNOT EAT RAW SPARKLEBUNNY.

DEAD PIRO DAY
MT PRINT VOLUME 3 "EXTRA" PREVIEW #2 OF
Endgames : Disabled

Darkwoods Pirogoeth

WHILE AT A-KON, I DID THIS LITTLE GIFT ART FOR JOHN KATZ (ARTIST BEHIND "LEGENDS OF DARKWOOD") IT CAME OUT REALLY NICE, SO I ASKED JOHN TO SCAN IT FOR ME SO I COULD SHARE IT. :)

THAT'S A UNICORN HORN, IN CASE YOU WERE WONDERING. BAD, BAD, BAD, PIROGOETH...

PIRO

OI, PIROGOETH
WHAT BE WITH
THE... SPIKE
THING?
06
05
04
FRED 'PIRO'
GALLAGHER

megatokyo gameworld

endgames

dead piro day freesketch

Pirogoeth - Queen of Kuith

STILL-ALIVE-AFTER-600-MT-STRIPS DEAD PIRO DAY SPECIAL

Upabove Station : LvP

ALWAYS WANTED TO DO A SCI-FI LARGO/PIRO GAMEWORLD THING. MY APOLOGIES TO CJ CHERRYH, MASAMUNE SHIROW, THE STELLVIA FOLKS, KEIJI GOTOH, THE AVP PEOPLE, JAMES P. HOGAN, WILLIAM GIBSON, AND... ER, WELL.. THE SCI-FI WORLD IN GENERAL
- PIRO -

Picnicing Darkly...

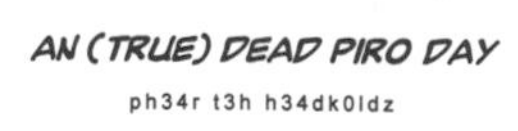

AN (TRUE) DEAD PIRO DAY
ph34r t3h h34dk0ldz

junpei

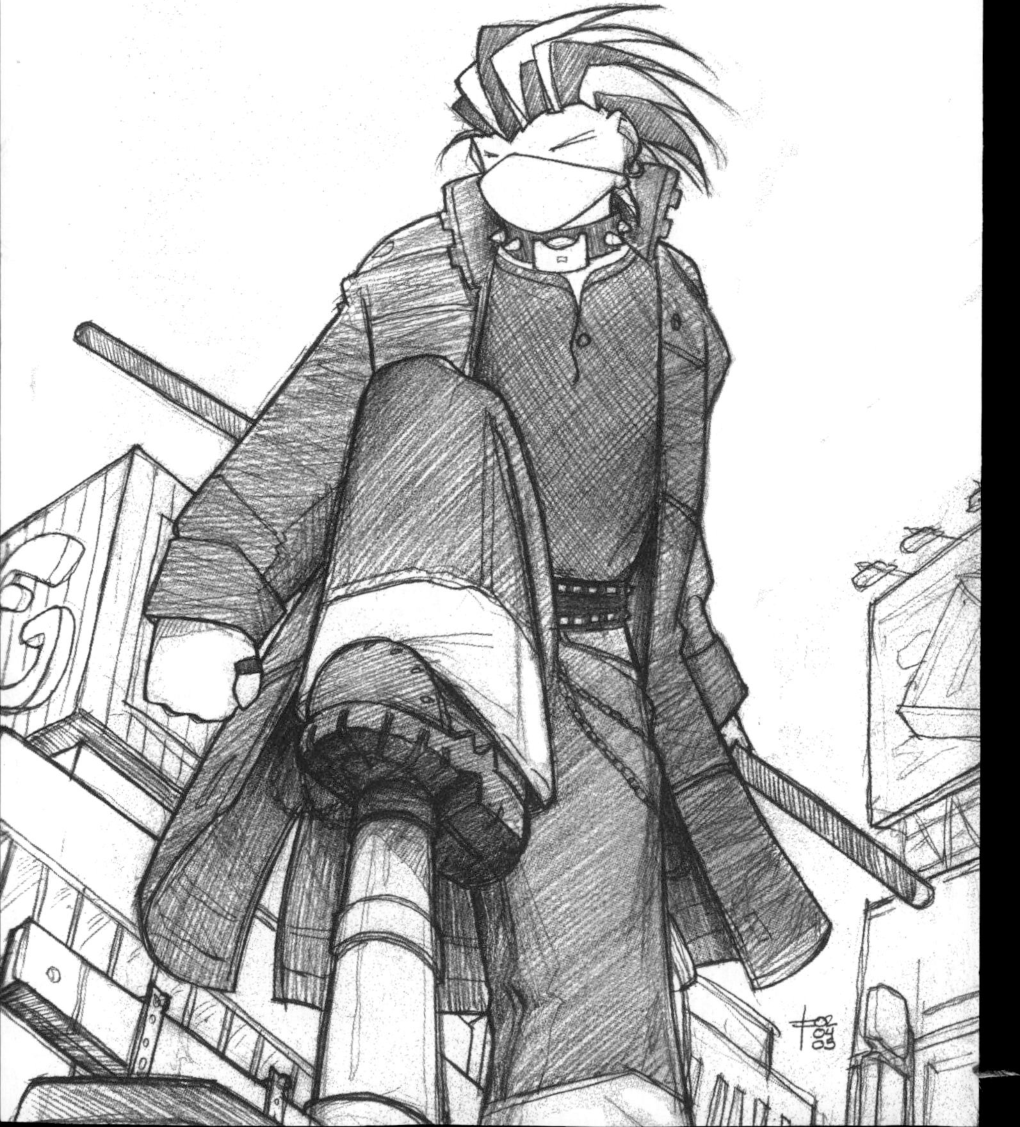

DEAD PIRO DAY FLASHBACK
"hmph."
FLASHBACK TO ERIKA WORKING AS KASUMI FROM DEAD OR ALIVE IN "ABUNAI BOOTHBABE" (COMIC #23). YES, I KNOW THE HAIR IS A LITTLE DIFFERENT, SO SUE ME. :P THE DRAWING IS A LITTLE OFF (WELL, A LOT OFF) BUT IT'S NOT TOO BAD.
PIRO

photoblog :: kumakuma
posted: saturday 09:45am
photograph of Nanasawa Kimiko, voice of Kannazuki Kotone in "Sight" she is very nice, very cute, and did not want her picture taken. i do not know why! she is very new, but seem to give all her heart to her performance! will try to get more pictures after recording session is over. I think you will like her!
kumakuma
01 05 05

end-of-chapter/its-a-holiday/not-feeling-funny-today/can-color-in-grays/just-a-sketch/moody-fredrin-day

DEAD PIRO DAY - FINDING YUKI

WE HAVEN'T SEEN YUKI AND HER FRIENDS FOR A WHILE - AND IT'S BEEN A LONG TIME SINCE I'VE DRAWN THEM. ALMOST WORSE THAN MY PROBLEM WITH KIMIKO, I "LOST" YUKI A LONG TIME AGO, AND RECENTLY I'VE BEEN WORKING ON FINDING HER CHARACTER AGAIN. THOSE EFFORTS AREN'T REFLECTED VERY WELL IN THIS DRAWING, BUT IT'S ANOTHER STEP ALONG THE PATH.

PIRO

SICK PIRO DAY ART LESSON

I FIGURED I'D DO SOMETHING A LITTLE DIFFERENT WITH THIS DPD/PREVIEW AND MAYBE GIVE A LITTLE LESSON / EXAMPLE OF COMIC LAYOUT STUFF. HEY, IT'S BETTER THAN STICK FIGURES, RIGHT? RIGHT.

NOW, TAKE A LOOK AT THESE TWO FRAMES, BOTH FROM DRAWINGS FOR THE NEXT COMIC (WHICH I AM WORKING ON, BUT ISN'T DONE YET):

THE DRAWING ON THE LEFT IS MY FIRST ATTEMPT AT FRAME ONE, WHERE PING IS ACCOSTING PIRO AND DEMANDS THAT HE STOP IGNORING HER. EVEN BEFORE I FINISHED THE DRAWING, I FELT THAT IT DIDN'T WORK WORK VERY WELL. I RETHOUGHT THE LAYOUT AND DID THE DRAWING OVER, RESULTING IN THE DRAWING ON THE RIGHT, WHICH IS WHAT I WILL ACTUALLY USE FOR FRAME ONE IN THE NEXT COMIC.

ONE OF THE THINGS ABOUT COMICS IS THAT EACH FRAME CONVEYS A CERTAIN AMOUNT OF TIME. WHEN CHARACTERS ARE MOVING OR THINGS ARE HAPPENING, YOU HAVE TO FRAME THINGS IN SUCH A WAY THAT IT'S CLEAR WHAT'S HAPPENING SO READERS CAN FOLLOW THE FLOW.

IN THIS FRAME, I NEEDED TO GIVE THE IMPRESSION THAT PIRO IS STILL WALKING ALONG SEEMINGLY DOWNCAST, WITH PING FOLLOWING HIM. SHE'S TRYING TO GET HIS ATTENTION, WORRIED ABOUT WHAT IS BOTHERING HIM. FINALLY, SHE SHOUTS HIS NAME IN FRUSTRATION, WHICH FINALLY BRINGS HIM TO A HALT.

THE FIRST FRAME WAS AN ATTEMPT TO SHOW PIRO AT THAT MOMENT WHERE PING SHOUTS OUT HIS NAME. IT'S A SNAPSHOT OF THE TAIL END OF THE 'MOMENT' THE FRAME COVERS. WITH NO FRAME BEFORE IT THAT SHOWS HIM MOPING, I DIDN'T THINK IT WORKED.

THE SECOND FRAME, WHICH IS MORE DYNAMIC, CLEARLY SHOW'S PIRO'S 'LOST IN THOUGHT' STAGGERING GAIT, AND THE SNAPSHOT POINT HERE IS REALLY IS WHEN PING STOPS AND YELLS OUT HIS NAME. IT IS A MOMENT BEFORE THE SURPRISED LOOK CAPTURED IN THE FIRST FRAME. I WONT BE BE SHOWING PIRO'S SURPRISED LOOK (THE NEXT FRAME WILL CUT TO SHOW PING, AND PERHAPS PIRO LOOKING AT HER) BUT I FELT THAT THE INFORMATION AND FLOW OF THE FRAME ON THE RIGHT WAS CLEARER AND CONVEYED THE STORY BETTER THAN THE ONE ON THE LEFT.

A GOOD COMIC, I THINK, IS ONE WHERE THE DRAWINGS AND THE DIALOGUE WORK TOGETHER TO CREATE A GOOD SENSE OF WATCHING THE STORY FLOW. YOUR DIALOGUE AND YOUR DRAWINGS DON'T HAVE TO SHOW THE SAME THING (FOR INSTANCE, IN THE LAST COMIC, PIRO DID NOT SAY 'HERE'S YOUR CELL PHONE' - THE DRAWING SHOWS HIM HANDING IT TO HER) AND YOU CAN USE CHARACTER'S EXPRESSIONS TO CONTRAST OR CONVEY THE TONE OF WHAT THEY ARE SAYING... AT ANY RATE, DON'T BE AFRAID TO PUT ASIDE A PERFECTLY GOOD DRAWING IF IT DOESN'T DO WHAT YOU NEED IT TO DO, EVEN IF YOU ARE SICK AND BEHIND AND END UP HAVING TO DO A LAME DPD...

(DISCLAIMER: I AM NO EXPERT, THIS IS JUST STUFF I'VE FIGURED OUT ON MY OWN, AND I HAVE NO IDEA IF IT REALLY WORKS OR IS JUST A BUNCH OF NONSENSE.)

"sad kimiko @ takaido station"

megatokyo
omake theater
presents...
circuity

tink
tink
tink
HOW FAR PAST THE EDGE OF THE WIND CAN SOMEONE GO BEFORE THEY ARE SWEPT AWAY?
WHY WOULD ANYONE EVER GO PAST THE EDGE?
THE WIND BEYOND THE EDGE NEVER STOPS.
IT IS A FEROCIOUS WIND THAT SWEEPS AWAY EVERYTHING IN ITS PATH.
A WIND THAT CAN RIP AWAY YOUR VERY SOUL.
IN THE DISTANCE YOU CAN SEE THE STUMPS AND BROKEN PIERS OF WINDMILLS DESTROYED BY THAT WIND.
EVEN WINDMILLS ON THIS SIDE OF THE EDGE SPIN AND BREAK WHEN THAT WIND TURNS THIS WAY.
ONLY A MADMAN WOULD EVER THINK OF GOING INTO THAT WIND.

THE WIND HAS TURNED THIS WAY.
A STORM IS COMING.
IF WE COULD PUSH IT BACK...
I THINK--
IT WOULDN'T WORK.
YOU CAN'T PUSH THE WIND.
THE WIND PUSHES THE BLADES AND MAKES THEM SPIN.
IF WE WERE TO SPIN THE BLADES, I AM SURE THEY WOULD PUSH THE WIND BACK.
RIGHT. SO HOW WOULD YOU DO THAT?
WE BARELY UNDERSTAND HOW THESE THINGS WORK, NEVERMIND CHANGING HOW THEY WORK.
DETAILS! I AM SURE THERE IS A WAY!
GREAT.
IF YOU DON'T MIND, I'D LIKE TO FINISH BEFORE THE STORM--
AH!
WHAT THE...

THERE'S SOMEONE--! LOOK OUT!!
REH?
fwip
fwip fwip
crack!
AH...
AH...
AHEEEEH....
I HIT HER!!
STOP!
AHHIIEEEEEH!!!
DO YOU NOT SEE THE WINGS?
DO NOT GO DOWN. SHE IS... THEY ARE...
STAY. I WILL GO DOWN.
LET GO OF ME.

SHE'S SHUDDERING--
KEEP HER STILL.
fwaf!
BLOOD LOSS. PAIN. SHOCK.
KEEP HER COVERED.
WITH WHAT? WE HAVE NO BLANKETS, AND THIS STORM IS MOVING IN FAST!!
THE CLOSEST SHELTER IS THE UTILITY BARN ON THE EDGE OF--
NO.
THEIR PLACE...
...IS MUCH CLOSER.
IS THIS IT?!? IT'S A RUIN!!
SHE IS THE FIRST ONE I'VE EVER SEEN...
AND I HURT HER.
WHAT SHOULD I DO? WE'RE NOT EVEN SUPPOSED TO--
WHERE IS SHE?
WHERE IS THE OTHER ONE??

WHERE IS SHE?!?
HEY!
BACK OFF!
WHAT'S YOUR PROBLEM?
THE OTHER ONE.
THIS IS HER ROOM. WHY ISN'T SHE HERE?
THE STORM... SHE MUST BE HERE! SHE ISN'T SAFE IF SHE ISN'T HERE!!
SHE SAID...
SHE HAD SOMETHING SHE HAD TO DO.
DAYS WENT BY AND SHE DIDN'T RETURN. THEN THERE WERE STORMS, AND A WIND THAT... THAT...
SHE... NEVER CAME BACK.
PLEASE DON'T BE SAD!
SHE TOLD ME ABOUT YOU! SHE MADE ME PROMISE NOT TO TELL YOU IF SHE EVER HAD TO...
GO AWAY.
RATTLE
RATTLE
RATTLE
I'LL GO START THE GENERATOR.
START A FIRE. THE CHILL CAN KILL THEM.

HHHOOOOOOWHOOOOOWHHHOOOOOO
I NEVER KNEW.

WE'VE BEEN PARTNERS FOR YEARS, FIXING WINDMILLS, DOING ELECTRICAL WORK.
HE'S NEVER MENTIONED HER BEFORE, NOT EVEN ONCE.
AND HE TALKS A LOT.

YES HE HAS.
HE TALKS ABOUT HER ALL THE TIME.
HE DOES?

WHENEVER HE TALKS ABOUT STOPPING THE AIR OR PUSHING BACK THE WIND...

HE IS TALKING ABOUT HER.

SO, CAN YOU FIX IT?

HEH.

CLUNDGHL
HUH.
I DIDN'T THINK THAT THING COULD BE FIXED.
SO, ARE THESE THINGS REAL?
CAN YOU FLY WITH 'EM?
FWAF!
WOW, THEY'RE SOFT.
TO ANSWER YOUR QUESTION, NO, I CAN'T FLY WITH THEM.
SO WHAT PURPOSE DO THEY SERVE?
FOR ME, NONE.
THEY ARE A BURDEN, AN INCONVENIENCE AND DANGER-OUS.
DANGER-OUS?
THINK ABOUT IT.
HAVING WINGS, LIVING ON THE EDGE OF THE WIND, WHERE EVEN ORDINARY PEOPLE CAN BE SWEPT AWAY IN A STORM...
THE WIND WILL FIND ME SOMEDAY. FOR MY KIND, IT ALWAYS DOES
KEEP THAT ICE ON YOUR EYE OR YOUR WHOLE HEAD WILL SWELL UP.

WHAT ARE YOU DOING?!?
DEFLECTING THE WIND!!
IF WINDMILL BLADES CAN CATCH THE WIND, THEY CAN DEFLECT IT TOO!!
THERE ARE THOUSANDS OF THESE SCATTERED AROUND!!
IF WE PUT UP ENOUGH OF THEM, THE WIND WILL NEVER BE ABLE TO REACH YOU!
NO!! PLEASE!!
JUST... STOP.
I KNOW YOU MEAN WELL.
JUST... STOP.
CLONG
TINK
TINK
SNICK

HHOOOOOWHOOOOOWHHOOOOO
THE STORM IS GETTING WORSE.
RATTLE RATTLE
RATTLE
HE'S BEEN GONE A LONG TIME. I HOPE HE'S OK.
RATTLE RATTLE
IT WAS SOON AFTER I CAME HERE...
HM?
...THAT SHE COULDN'T SEE HIM ANYMORE.
A WEEK LATER... SHE WAS GONE.
I HAD HOPED... THAT SHE HAD GONE TO HIM. BUT WHEN I WENT AND LISTENED TO HIM WORK... I KNEW...SHE WAS GONE.
ALL I HAD LEFT WAS HER JOURNAL.
I BEGAN TO WRITE WHAT HE SAID IN IT... WHAT HE SAID TO YOU... SO THAT SHE COULD HEAR TOO...
SO THEY COULD STILL BE CLOSE...
FOR OVER A YEAR, I LISTENED TO THE VOICES FROM ABOVE, AND WROTE DOWN WHAT THEY SAID.
BUT... I HAVE TO GO SOON.
I CAN FEEL IT.
THAT'S WHY I WAS THERE... WAITING FOR YOU, AT THE BASE OF THE MILL.
I WANTED... TO GIVE IT TO HIM... SO HE COULD KEEP TALKING TO HER.
AND TO MEET YOU... THE OTHER VOICE.
I WANTED TO... BEFORE I...
I DON'T WANT TO GO...
SHH.
YOU DON'T HAVE TO GO ANY-WHERE. REST.
shff

I DON'T WANT TO GO...
WHHHOOOOOOWHOOOOOWHHHOOO
WHHHOOOOOOWHOOOOOOWHHHOOOO

WAKE.
UWEH?
IT IS MORNING. THE STORM HAS QUIETED.
IT HAS? GOOD.
I WAS BEGINNING TO WORRY.
AND YOU! WHAT TOOK--
NO...

NO.

WE CAN'T JUST LEAVE HER HERE...
LIKE THIS...
WE CAN'T...
WHAT WAS THAT??
CRASH!
FWIP
WUMP
WHERE ARE YOU?!?

FWOOM!
WHAT ARE YOU DOING?!?
FWOOM!
SO YOU JUST LET IT TAKE YOU?
YOU DON'T EVEN FIGHT IT??
FWOOM
I SAID I WOULD PUSH BACK THE WIND FOR YOU!

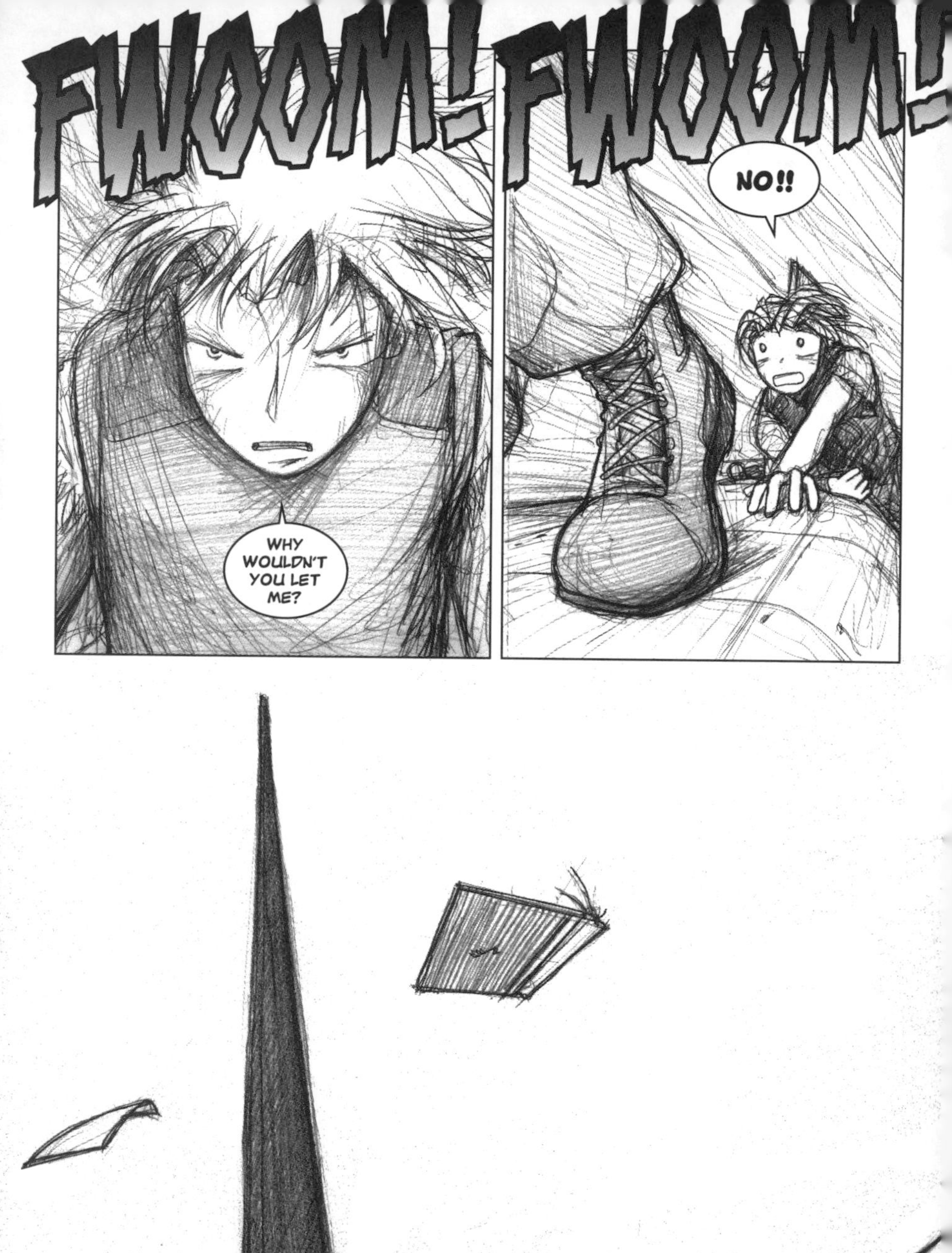
FWOOM!
WHY WOULDN'T YOU LET ME?
FWOOM!
NO!!

TO PUSH BACK THE WIND...
IS SUCH A THING EVEN POSSIBLE?
TO CHANGE THE WAY IT BLOWS, TO FORCE IT BACK.
TO NOT ACCEPT WHAT IT BRINGS.
I, TOO WANT TO PUSH IT BACK...
BUT I AM TOO AFRAID TO TRY.
END.

megatokyo omake theater hopes
you have enjoyed this "rewound" presentation of

circuity

Megatokyo - Volume 4 index

This book contains strips from Chapter 5, Chapter 6 and includes extra material produced between February 2003 and August 2005. For more information and more comics, visit www.megatokyo.com

Page No.	Strip Title	Date	Online Strip ID
92	such a silly idea	2004-10-06	618
93	still a mess in here	2004-10-08	619
94	2wo ch1x0rz	2004-10-08	620
95	going away	2004-10-13	621
96	flirting and cleaning	2004-10-15	622
97	are you capable of playing this?	2004-10-18	623
98	Who do you play?	2004-10-22	625
99	they want to be free!	2004-10-25	626
100	a mismatched pair	2004-10-27	627
101	finding happiness where you can	2004-10-29	628
102	Shipping methods	2004-11-01	629
103	mashing buttons	2004-11-05	631
104	toasting the end of a long day	2004-11-08	632
105	measurable progress	2004-11-10	633
106	Fashion Trip around the World!	2004-11-22	638

Chapter 06

Page No.	Strip Title	Date	Online Strip ID
107	Chapter 6: Operational Insecurity	2004-11-24	639
108	ph34r of head injuries	2004-11-29	641
109	intimidation	2004-12-01	642
110	wanting to know more about you	2004-12-03	643
111	open your eyes	2004-12-06	644
112	please stop	2004-12-16	648
113	i will do it myself	2004-12-20	649
114	pre-assembled abominations	2004-12-22	650
115	so sweet	2004-12-24	651
116	cute frenetic panic	2004-12-27	652
117	static can be deadly	2004-12-29	653
118	cute little gym shorts	2004-12-31	654
119	don't want to think about it	2005-01-03	655
120	270 seconds	2005-01-07	657
121	really soft	2005-01-10	658
122	there is no luck	2004-01-12	659
123	pretty girl discount	2005-01-14	660
124	missed calls	2005-01-17	661
125	expressing obsessions	2005-01-19	662
126	say what you feel	2005-01-21	663
127	i don't want to ruin it	2005-01-24	664
128	afraid?	2005-01-26	665
129	a commodity	2005-01-28	666
130	please be there	2005-01-31	667
131	low load limit	2005-02-02	668
132	probably busy anyway	2005-02-07	670
133	a lot to do	2005-02-09	671
134	hiding in plain sight	2005-02-11	672
135	bargain shopping	2005-02-14	673
136	honor much safer	2005-02-16	674
137	such a serious young man	2005-02-18	675
138	losing sense of feeling	2005-02-21	676
139	some expert	2005-02-24	678
140	showing interest	2005-02-25	679
141	something for me	2005-02-28	680
142	damage was taken	2005-03-02	681
143	ice cubes	2005-03-04	682
144	crazy talk	2005-03-07	683
145	not very good at it	2005-03-09	684
146	chatty little thing	2005-03-11	685
147	so play already	2005-03-14	686
148	friend check	2005-03-16	687
149	you gonna play or you gonna whine?	2005-03-18	688
150	the desire to drink yourself numb	2005-03-21	689
151	voice mail	2005-03-23	690
152	you'll dance with me, won't you?	2005-04-01	693
153	Into The Darkest Void	2005-04-04	694
154	no sad girls on my show!	2005-04-06	695
155	rejection recovery	2005-04-11	696
156	some time to talk	2005-04-13	697
157	something old and unopened	2005-04-15	698
158	i don't think you should listen	2005-04-18	699
159	poor fanboy	2005-04-20	700
160	a fanboy's fears	2005-04-22	701
161	rejection beliefs	2005-04-25	702
162	small sips	2005-04-27	703
163	in clubs, no one can hear you scream	2005-04-29	704
164	warmer	2005-05-02	705
165	caring	2005-05-04	706
166	torn	2005-05-06	707
167	weapon trails	2005-05-11	709
168	certain death	2005-05-16	710
169	not taking it very well	2005-05-18	711
170	the perfect kill	2005-05-20	712
171	you might get hurt	2005-05-23	713
172	doomed	2005-05-25	714
173	i cannot heal if i cannot get away	2005-05-27	715
174	safe	2005-05-30	716
175	i have my reasons	2005-06-01	717
176	it never really healed quite right	2005-06-03	718
177	a lot like you	2005-06-08	720
178	finding fault	2005-06-10	721
179	'yer better'n dat	2005-06-13	722
180	why do you say these things?	2005-06-15	723
181	already broken	2005-06-17	724
182	letting things happen	2005-06-20	725
183	damage control	2005-06-22	726
184	how was your day?	2005-06-24	727
185	don't want to scare him away	2005-06-29	728
186	it was a good day	2005-07-01	729
187	Leave it to Seraphim! - Earth Friendly Fashions	2005-08-01	742

ELCOME TO THE NEW WORLD OF CMX!

e hope you have enjoyed this latest edition of MEGATOKYO! this is your first CMX book, or if you just haven't checked us ut in a while, please take a look at these other new and pcoming manga releases.

VS. (Versus)

By Keiko Yamada *(Drama)*

At a prestigious music school, a fiery teacher helps a troubled violin prodigy to achieve his dreams.

On sale now.

Oyayubihime Infinity

By Toru Fujieda *(Comedy)*

A group of reincarnated friends tries to reconcile past connections with present desires.

On sale now.

Omukae Desu

By Meca Tanaka *(Comedy)*

A boy who can see dead people joins an agency that helps them cross over to the other side.

On sale August 2006.

The Recipe for Gertrude

By Nari Kusakawa *(Comedy)*

A young girl helps a man-made demon to elude his enemies and find the formula that created him.

On sale August 2006.

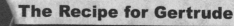

Page No.	Strip Title	Date	Onlin
	Shirt Guy Dom Strips		
190	SGD: Ed's social graces	2004-05-28	564
191	SGD: Uneasy is the Head...	2005-03-28	691
192	SGD: Crossed Wires	2005-07-27	740
	One-Shot (non-story) Episodes		
193	Meanwhile...Dom Sings Barry!	2004-12-10	646
194	Meanwhile...A wish for rockets that work	2004-12-08	645
195	OSE - mail from home	2004-04-19	549
196	endgames - depopulation and wayfinding	2004-09-13	608
197	OSE: endgames::groupattack	2004-11-19	637
198	Seraphim's Live Journal Theater	2004-07-02	579
199	OSE: Adventures in running your own biz!	2004-11-15	635
200	Piro & Seraphim Run Away (never posted)		
	Dead Piro Art Days		
202	DPD: Endgames preview - sparklebunny burning	2004-11-12	634
203	DPD: Endgames preview - Fougoureth	2004-11-26	640
204	DPD: Darkwoods Pirogoeth	2004-06-07	568
205	DPD: Pirogoeth - Queen of Kuith	2005-05-09	708
206	Upabove Station - LvP	2004-08-25	600
207	DPD - picnicking darkly	2004-06-01	565
208	DPD: Junpei	2005-02-04	669
209	DPD: Hmph.	2004-10-20	624
210	DPD: Photoblog:Kumakuma	2005-01-05	656
211	DPD: finding yuki	2005-06-06	719
212	DPD: Sick Piro Day Art Lesson #1	2005-02-23	677
213	DPD: Sad Kimiko @ Takaido Station	2004-11-03	630
214	DPD: painting in grays	2005-07-04	730
	Circuity *		
215-233	Megatokyo Omake Theater: Circuity	2005-07-06	731
	Circuity: pushing the wind	2005-07-08	732
	Circuity: cursed	2005-07-11	733
	Circuity: the other one	2005-07-13	734
	Circuity: never came home	2005-07-15	735
	Circuity: voices from above	2005-07-18	736
	Circuity: gone	2005-07-20	737
	Circuity: pushed by the wind	2005-07-21	738
	Circuity: loss	2005-07-25	739
	Circuity: curtain call	2005-07-29	741

* Note: Circuity has been extensively rewritten and expanded for this book. The online version (listed here) is still available to read in its original form.